Alexander The Great

Incorporating Alexander the Great and the Defeat

(*An Epic Novel of the Decline and Death of Alexander the Great)*

Teresa Drain

Published By **Regina Loviusher**

Teresa Drain

All Rights Reserved

Alexander The Great: Incorporating Alexander the Great and the Defeat (An Epic Novel of the Decline and Death of Alexander the Great)

ISBN 978-1-77485-538-6

No part of this guidebook shall be reproduced in any form without permission in writing from the publisher except in the case of brief quotations embodied in critical articles or reviews.

Legal & Disclaimer

The information contained in this ebook is not designed to replace or take the place of any form of medicine or professional medical advice. The information in this ebook has been provided for educational & entertainment purposes only.

The information contained in this book has been compiled from sources deemed reliable, and it is accurate to the best of the Author's knowledge; however, the Author cannot guarantee its accuracy and validity and cannot be held liable for any errors or omissions. Changes are periodically made to this book. You must consult your doctor or get professional medical advice before using any of the suggested remedies, techniques, or information in this book.

Upon using the information contained in this book, you agree to hold harmless the Author from and against any damages, costs, and expenses, including any legal fees potentially resulting from the application of any of the information provided by this guide. This disclaimer applies to any damages or injury caused by the use and application, whether directly or indirectly, of any advice or information presented, whether for breach of contract, tort, negligence, personal injury, criminal intent, or under any other cause of action.

You agree to accept all risks of using the information presented inside this book. You need to consult a professional medical practitioner in order to ensure you are both able and healthy enough to participate in this program.

TABLE OF CONTENTS

Introduction

Chapter 1: Ancient Macedon

Chapter 2: Childhood, And Youth

Chapter 3: The Beginning Of His Reign

Chapter 4: Battle Of Persia

Chapter 5: Moving Forward To Issus

Chapter 6: The Siege Of Tyre

Chapter 7: Alexander In Egypt

Chapter 8: Battle Of Gaugamela. Battle Of Gaugamela

Chapter 9: Pursuit Of Darius

Chapter 10: To All The End Of The Earth

Chapter 11: A Return To Persia

Chapter 12: Susa Marriages

Chapter 13: Crossing The Hellespont

Chapter 14: A Campaign Asia Minor

Chapter 15: Alexander's Final

Conclusion

Introduction

Alexander III of Macedon died at just 32 in 323 BC. He was a king for just 13 years, and was the heir to an unimportant kingdom at the northern side of Greece. He transformed the tiny Macedonian kingdom Macedon into the most powerful state of Greece and later defeated the biggest empire ever known.

He was hailed as "The Great" due to his military genius and his incredible feats of victory, however the man was also an incredible persona. He believed he was the child of Zeus He was adored and adored by his soldiers who battled side-by-side with in all of his most ferocious battles. He was able to accomplish through determination and determination what appeared to be unattainable.

Alexander revolutionized the direction of the world, in bringing his native Middle East and Egypt into the Greek world and spreading "Hellenism" which is Greek culture of arts exploring theatre, literature music, architecture and mathematics. He also introduced philosophy, mathematics and science to its fullest extent.

Alexander III from Macedon is among those people who have changed historical events. He is deservedly referred to as Alexander the Great.

Chapter 1: Ancient Macedon

Ancient Macedon is situated in the area that is now Northern Greece and the Former Yugoslav Republic of Macedonia. It was situated on the Northern part of Ancient Greece and was not a nation within the contemporary sense, but there were a few tiny, independent city-states, that were inhabited by Greek natives. The most famous among them include Athens, Corinth and Sparta.

This group of Greeks view their northern neighbors as a barbaric, backward kingdom that was awash with hunting and drinking, in contrast to the more democratic culturally educated Athenians. This was the backwater of agriculture that Alexander's father took over as the leader of the Argead Dynasty in 359 BC.

Alexander's father Phillip II Phillip II

Phillip was just 23 when he ascended to the throne and was trying in the process of establishing his position in the throne, and was still afloat in the throne. His first priority was to protect his borders and to reform the army.

Phillip managed to establish his authority while his southern neighbors were focusing on other issues, during the civil conflict. Phillip's focus was on changing the army into the best army of the time. In the beginning, Phillip was focused exclusively on infantry. When he was a young man, Phillip was taken hostage by the city state of Thebes. In a bid to understand what he saw, the pattern he chose to use, it was called Theban wedge. Theban wedge, also known as the an echelon. The wedge was made up of columns that protruded and arranged up to 50 shields in depth. It proved to be an extremely powerful weapon. Philip transformed the weaponry from a hoplite spear to a the sarissa, which was an 18 up to 20-foot pike, more than double the length of traditional weapon. Sarissa had the additional benefit of having at minimum four spear points protruding from the between the shield of his front. None of the hoplite armies in the present were equipped to handle these new developments. Sarissa heads alone measured two feet, and cut through armor and shields, as swords that were attached to wooden poles. The opponent's hoplite who's shield was affixed and dislocated by one of the sarissa quickly became bloody by a different.

Philip also altered his helmets, and redesigned the shields and every man was also given a smaller, double-edged sword, an xiphos to combat hand-to-hand. The changes, along with significant drilling changed the Macedonian phalanx to be the most equipped, well-drilled and highly tactically superior around the globe.

During Alexander's campaigns , the Phalanx was not utilized as the primary weapon, but was reserved for the second arm, which Philip transformed into the cavalry. The Phalanx was Alexander's strike weapon. His cavalry was to be the first "shock" weapon that date back to antiquity. At the time, the stirrups were not invented, and horses were not equipped with the right support to use heavy weaponry or precisely pointed bows. The majority of cavalry units were equipped with javelins and lances. Moving within the distance of enemy troops, they would attack and weaken the infantry of the enemy before the phalanx would lead the main assault.

Phillip changed the Macedonian cavalry to make the most of their greater mobility. The cavalry mounted soldiers were taught to become skilled horsemen who were able to control their horses and remain on the battlefield to battle on horseback in close spaces. Phillip also modified the normal arrangement to a wedge instead of an arranged block. This increased mobility and the shock of cavalry. The wedge narrowed , making it a point to pierce the enemy's formations. It's simpler to turn than a square-shaped formation since everyone followed the leader to the point of the apex. The cavalry also performed the crucial task of ensuring that the phalanx did not get out of the flanks.

The most terrorized in the army of cavalry were the Companion cavalry since they were the Companions of Alexander. They were typically placed on the right of the phalanx.

This army was the key to Philip II's expanding control over Greek city-states in the south. Philip was able triumph in a variety of combats against the enemies such as Thessaly in 353 BC, the Phoecians at the Battle of Crocus Field in 352 and the most important one, the alliance between the Athenian as well as Thebes army in The Battle of Chaeronea during 388. This enabled Philip to establish the League which was named Corinth in 337BC. This was later called"the" Hellenic League. The league was an association of Greek states established by Philip II following the battle of Chaeronea to aid in the use of military troops during his battle against Persia. Each member of the league was required to take the identical swearing. The inscription that was discovered in Athens:

Oath. "I swear to Zeus, Gaia, Helios, Poseidon and all the gods and goddesses. I will keep the peace of the commons and will not break the contract with Philip or to take up arms either on the sea or land and harm any one who abide by the swearings. Do not I invade any fortress, city or town or harbor by means of craft or ingenuity, with the intentions of war against participants in the conflict. Also, I shall not depose the monarchy from Philip and his offspring, or the constitutions of each state when they took the oaths to keep peace. And I shall not act against these treaties or let anyone else do so much as is possible. If anyone is found to be in any violation or violation of this treaty, then I will help as demanded by those in need. I will take on the violators in the name of peace according to the decision (by the Council) and urged by the hegemon, and I will not leave --------"

Philip planned to use this league to take on Persia, the great empire that was to the east. The king would never have this chance since his death in 336BC was committed by a court official who was just a few years old Pausanias. It would be an 18-year-old Alexander who succeeded him, but let's look back a bit and examine how Alexander came to where he is today.

Chapter 2: Childhood, And Youth

B.C. 356-336

The short life of Alexander's career The Shortness of Alexander's Career Alexander the Great died while it was a very young man. He was only thirty-two years of age at the time he ended his professional career. And as it was around twenty years old when began his career in the first place, it was for a total of twelve years during which he was working on the tasks that shaped his entire life. Napoleon was three times longer on the vast world of human action.

His amazing Exploits - Despite the time-strapped nature of Alexander's life it was not without a flurry of within a short time span an extremely brilliant sequence of adventures, that were both so daring and romantic, and that took to such thrilling adventures, in scenes of incredible magnificence and splendorthat people around the world watched with amazement. The world has continued to follow the tale since then as they grew older with great interest and interest.

The personality of Alexander. Physical and Mental Qualities The secret to Alexander's success was his personality. Alexander was a unique mix of personal and mental attraction that in all ages people who display it with a mysterious and unlimited power over others under their reach. Alexander was distinguished by these traits in a extraordinary way. He was a well-rounded his appearance, and was very opulent in his conduct. He was athletic, active and full of enthusiasm and passion in everything his activities. However he was calm and well-organized, and considerate of situations that required caution. He was also attentive and observant in regard to the implications and bearings of his actions. He was a strong ally and was thankful for the kindnesses given by others, thoughtful with regard toward the opinions of those people who were related to his in any way, loyal to his family and friends and generous to those he opposed. In a nutshell his character was noble. persona, yet he devoted his energies to defeat and war. He was a man of in a time when immense mental and physical power could not find a better place to exercise their power that this. He began his profession with enthusiasm and the position at the job he held allowed him to carry out his work with great success.

The nature of Asiatic character of the Asiatic and European Civilization - There were various circumstances that were combined with the circumstances in which Alexander was put, to give him an excellent opportunity to use his immense power. His country of birth was situated in the midst to Europe as well as Asia. Today, Europe as well as Asia were at the time, just as they are today separated and marked by two massive populations of civilized and social living, vastly different from one another. The Asiatic part was occupied by Persians as well as the Medes along with the Assyrians. The European part was occupied by Greeks along with the Romans. These two groups were separated from one from each other by the waters of the Hellespont and The AEgean Sea, and the Mediterranean as evident from the map. These waters were a form of natural barrier that kept the two races separate. The two races grew into two massive organizations distinct and vastly different from one another and of course, competitors and adversaries.

Comprised of Asiatic and European Armies The European armies were composed of Asiatic and European troops. It is not easy to decide if either the Asiatic or European civilization was the most advanced. Both were so distinct that it's hard to make a comparison between them. The Asiatic side was wealth, luxury and splendor, while on the other hand, on European the other, there was energy, creativity and strength. On one hand, there were huge cities, magnificent gardens and palaces that were the most beautiful in the world. On the other hand, solid citadels with military road, bridges, as well as towns that were compact and well-defended. The Persians had massive armies fully stocked with magnificent tents, magnificently caparisoned horses as well as arms and munitions from military excellence and officers who were elegantly dressed and used to an era of splendor and luxury. They Greeks and Romans however, in contrast, boasted of their small-sized troops, accustomed to the rigors of battle and well-trained. Their leaders were not interested in extravagant parades and luxury instead, but in the bravery and the steadfastness the implicit obedience of their troops as well as in their own knowledge of skill, ability, and the power of military calculations. There was a huge distinction in the entire system of military and social organisation in these two regions of the world.

Then Alexander was born as the next heir to the throne in an of Grecian kingdoms. He had, to an astonishing way of energy, ambition, and military expertise that was characteristic of Greeks as well as the Romans. He commanded army units, crossed the border that separated Europe and Asia and spent the 12 years of his career engaged in an extremely successful military expedition into the heart and the seat of Asiatic power, taking down his Asiatic armies, and capturing the most beautiful cities, and abducting the kings and princes, as well as generals who opposed his efforts. Everyone was awestruck in amazement at an enactment of conquer, executed so effectively by a young a person, and with such a small army, and gaining constant victories in the process over such large numbers of adversaries, and making victories over such treasures of riches and glory.

King Philip. The extent of Macedon. Olympias is the name given to the father of Alexander was Philip. The kingdom the king ruled was named Macedon. Macedon was located in the northern portion of Greece. It was a kingdom that was twice as big as the Commonwealth of Massachusetts and one third bigger than New York State. New York. The mother of Alexander's was Olympias. Her father was King Epirus which was a kingdom that was smaller than Macedon and located west of it. It is believed that both Macedon and Epirus can be seen on the map in the beginning the volume. Olympias is a lady who had a extremely strong and determined personality. Alexander was believed to have inherited her determination, although the case of Alexander was paired with other characteristics that made him a better person that his mother didn't possess.

The Prince Young Alexander The Young Prince Alexander was of course as the young prince and a highly important figure within the court of his father. Everyone was aware that upon the death of his father, the prince would be crowned the King of Macedon and was the subject of lots of attention and attention. As he progressed through during his childhood It was noted by those whom he met that he infused with exceptional abilities of mind and personality that seemed to be a sign, even in a very young age, the potential for his greatness.

The Ancient Method of Warfare While he was a prince but he wasn't raised in a culture of affluence and luxury. This would have been in opposition to the notions that were embraced by the Greeks at the time. They did not have fire-arms and, in battle, the soldiers could not sit still, as they do today, at a distance from the enemy, stoically firing musketry or cannon. In the battles of old, the soldiers would rush towards each other and fought hand in hand during close combat, using spears, swords, or other weapons that demanded great personal strength. As a result, strong and ruthless courage were the characteristics that typically prevailed.

Modern and Ancient Military Officers The duties of officers also, on the battlefield of battle, were different as they are today. Officers today should be calm, composed and calm. The role of an officer involves planning, determine, to control and plan. It is his job to plan, calculate, direct and arrange often; that's the truth when he is in most imminent threat, which means that he has to be a person of tremendous self-confidence and unflinching determination. There isn't much chance for him to use the force of a great physique.

In the past but the main task of officers, particularly in the subordinate ranks were to guide the men and show them the way by executing actions in which their individual skills were displayed. Naturally, it was crucial that a youngster who would become general be strong and strong in the earliest age and be awed by hardship and fatigue. Early in Alexander's time, this was the primary focus of his attention.

Alexander's Nurse. Alexander's Education. Lysimachus is the Name of the nursing assistant who was in the charge of our hero during his infant years was Lannice. She was able to do everything she could to impart the strength and toughness to his constitution. At the same time she also her treatment of him was respect and kindness. Alexander developed a deep affection for her, and was a great lover of her for the duration of his life. He had a governor also in his young years, named Leonnatus, who was in charge of the overall responsibility for his education. Once he was sufficiently educated and become as a preceptor, in addition to teach him the branches that were taught to princes of the young in the days of. The name of the Preceptor was Lysimachus.

Homer The time was when there were no printed books. However, there were some written works on parchment rolls that students could be taught. There were philosophical works or romantic histories that recounted the adventures of the heroes of the past with a lot of extravagant and exaggerated. There were also poems that were more romantic than the stories, but they were generally on the same subject. The most popular examples of this were those written by Homer the poet of old who wrote and lived about five hundred years prior to Alexander's time. Alexander was a young Alexander was extremely impressed by the stories of Homer. These stories are narrated of the adventures and triumphs of some great warriors during the battle of Troy, a one-year-long siege, and they are written with such power and beauty They contain such beautiful descriptions of characters, and the most vivid and graphic description of romance as well as stunning and beautiful scenes that they are admired throughout the ages by everyone who've learned the languages in which they are written.

Aristotle. Alexander's Copy of Homer The Homer of Alexander's Copy Alexander was able to comprehend them easilysince these were written in his native language. He was extremely enthralled by the narratives and was awed by the smooth flow of text in which the stories were presented. The latter half of his education, He was put under the direction of Aristotle who was considered to be considered to be one of the more prominent philosophers of the past. Aristotle was the proud owner of a gorgeous version of Homer's poems written specifically for Alexander who took great care to translate it perfectly with the highest quality and beautiful way. Alexander carried the copy in all of his battles. A few years later, as the Persians were gaining victories, the Persians and the Persians, he gathered, as a reward for one of the victories, an extremely expensive and beautiful casket which the king Darius was using to store his jewelry or various other items. Alexander decided to use the container as a storage space for his exquisite version of Homer and always carried it around with his, thus ensuring its safety during his subsequent battles.

Alexander's energy and Ambition Alexander was filled with enthusiasm and spirit, yet Alexander was in the same way as all those who achieve greatness, possessed of an introspective and sensitive mind. Alexander was extremely enthusiastic about the research that Aristotle encouraged his attention to, even though they were of an complicated and complex nature. He made significant advancements in metaphysical philosophy as well as math, which meant that his calculation skills and judgement were greatly enhanced.

He showed early a tremendous level of ambition. Philip was his father. Philip was a formidable warriorwho made numerous conquers across Greece but Philip did not venture into Asia. When news of Philip's victories made it to Macedon, the other court would be filled with celebration and joy; however, Alexander during such events was silent and dejected and complained that Philip would be the one to take over every nation, and leave him with nothing to accomplish.

The Persian Embassadors. The stories of Embassadors There was a time when embassadors of the Persian court came to Macedon while Philip was absent. They met Alexander obviously and were able to speak to Alexander. They anticipated that he'd be interested in learning about the magnificence, the pomp and show and parades of the Persian monarchy. They had tales to tell regarding the famed hanging gardens that were constructed artificially in the most stunning way, using arches that were raised up in the air and also about a vine that was that was made of gold and many precious stones on the vine instead of fruits, made to be an ornament on the throne where The King of Persia frequently entertained his audience. of the magnificent palaces and huge cities of the Persians and feasts, banquets, and extravagant celebrations and entertainments that they would have there. However, they discovered to their shock, Alexander did not seem interested in all of this. Alexander would often turn the conversation and inquire into the geographic location of the various Persian countries, the numerous routes to an interior region, the organisation of Asiatic army, the method of combat tactics, and particularly, the personality and behavior of Artaxerxes the Persian King.

The maturity of Alexander's mind - The ambassadors were amazed by the evidence of mental maturity as well as of a keen-eyed and reflective capabilities on the part the prince's younger brother. They couldn't resist comparing his qualities with Artaxerxes. "Alexander," said they, "is great, while our king is only wealthy." The reality of the opinion the embassadors then formed with regard to the virtues that the new Macedonian as compared to those considered the best in his Asiatic part, verified in the following phases of Alexander's life.

Alexander's Secret. Alexander's Success. Story of Bucephalus - In the real world, this combination of a calm and calculated thinking, coupled with the passion and enthusiasm that formed the foundation of his character was the key to Alexander's great success. The tale of Bucephalus the famous horse illustrates this in a stunning way. Bucephalus was a war horse that was very energetic and was sent as a gift to Philip when Alexander was still a young. The horse was brought out into one of the gardens associated with the palace as the King, along with his courtiers took a stroll to see the horse. The horse sprinted around in a frenzied manner and appeared to be completely uncontrollable. There was no one who dared to mount him. Philip rather than being happy at the moment is more likely to be unhappy by the fact that they sent him an animal that was so fierce and evidently vicious that no one dares to control him.

At the same time when all of the others in the crowd were participating in condemning horses, Alexander remaining silently by looking at his movements and with a keen eye on his personality. He realized that a large part of the issue resulted from the anxiety that the horse was experiencing in such unusual and novel a setting and the horse appeared at times, to be a bit scared by his shadow which was at the time to fall very hard and clearly onto the ground. There were other signs as well, indicating that the excitement the horse experienced was not violent, but rather the result of an excess of generous and noble emotions. It was passion, courage and the awareness of a tremendous muscular and nervous strength.

Philip is adamant about the Horse. Alexander wants to mount him. Philip had concluded that the horse was ineffective and had issued instructions to send him back to Thessaly from where he had come. Alexander was deeply concerned about losing such a fine animal. Alexander begged his father for permission to try taking him on. Philip initially was hesitant, believing it to be foolish for a young man to try to control an animal that was so vicious that his grooms and horsemen condemned his efforts, but Philip eventually agreed. Alexander approached the horse, and took him by the hand the bridle. He brushed him on the neck and reassured him with his words and showed that, simultaneously with his calm and relaxed manner that he wasn't in the least fear of his. A horse with a lot of energy is aware that someone is approaching him in a cautious or timid way. The horse appears to gaze at such an owner, and decide not to bow to him. In contrast horses appear to be eager to bow to human in cases where the person who enforces obedience has the traits of coolness and courage that their instincts allow them to recognize.

Alexander and Bucephalus

Bucephalus calmed. An Exciting Ride all times, Bucephalus was calmed and calmed by Alexander's presence. Alexander. He let himself be touched. Alexander turned his head so to block his shadow. He laid down quietly and gently on a kind of clothing he wore and then put it on the back of the horse. Then, rather than trying to hold him back, or stressing and squeezing him with unsuccessful efforts to keep him back, he let the rein to him freely and enthused and enthused him by speaking, which caused the horse to fly over the open plains on the speed of his speed with the courtiers and the king looking on, initially in fear and nervousness and then soon afterwards with feelings of utmost satisfaction and admiration. After the horse was content with himself with his performance, it was simple to control him and Alexander returned with his horse in peace to the King. The courtiers were awestruck by their praises and congratulation. Philip gave him a high recommendation and told him that the kingdom he was destined to rule was much bigger than Macedon to run.

Bucephalus's Sagacity. The horse that became Alexander's favorite Alexander's assessment of the character the horse proved accurate. He was able to be handled and calm, giving complete obedience to his master at all times. He would sit on his front legs under Alexander's commands, so to ride more quickly. Alexander kept him for a lengthy period making him his preferred war horse. Many stories are shared by the historians of those times of his skill and feats of combat. If he was in the battlefield by his military equipment and equipment, he appeared to be extremely euphoric with joy and pride and, at these times his only desire was for anyone other than Alexander to be his mount.

The fate of Bucephalus What happened to his final fate isn't certain. There are two theories of his death. One of them is that on one moment Alexander was dragged into the arms of his foes in a battlefield and after fighting for a while, Bucephalus made the most difficult efforts to take him off. He was wounded repeatedly time and again, but even though his strength was dwindling however, he refused to stop in his tracks, and continued to push forward until the horse had carried his master to a safe place and then fell down exhausted and passed away. It is possible, however it is possible that he didn't actually die in this moment however, but slowly recovered as some historians claim that he lived until he was thirty years old, which is an high standard for a horse. It is also believed that he passed away. Alexander was able to have him cremated with great ceremony and erected a small city around the grave in honor in his honor. The city's name was Bucephalia.

Alexander Was made Regent The character of Alexander grew quickly and he began early to assume the character of man. He was just sixteen years old his grandfather, Philip, made him regent of Macedon even though he was in a major military battle with the different states in Greece. It is certain that Alexander was able to count on, during this regency, the advice and assistance of senior officers of state with a lot of expertise and experience. However, he acted himself in this important position with great energy and with great accomplishment; and in the same way wearing all the elegance of his appearance and the delicate consideration for the officers in his midst, who even though they were lower in rank, nevertheless were his superiors in terms of age and experience. His position made acceptable, yet only a handful of people as young as he were would have displayed in circumstances as designed to evoke emotions of pride and happiness.

Alexander's First Battle. Chaeronea - Following that when Alexander was around 18 years old young his father took him his father on a trip to the south. During this campaign, Philip was involved in one of his greatest battles at Chaeronea which was located in Boeotia. When preparing for this battle Philip granted the charge on one of the wings his army to Alexander as well as he kept the other one for him. Philip was a bit enthused about giving his son this important a task, however he was determined to protect himself from the possibility of a disastrous outcome by placing the most competent generals to Alexander's side, and he reserving those whom he would place little reliance on to his own. The army was then organized and began to battle.

Philip was soon to cease feeling any resentment for Alexander's portion of the responsibility. As a boy his age, the prince performed with the most ferocious elegance, and shrewdness. The wing that he was directing was victorious. Philip was forced to push his officers and him to exert more effort to ensure that he did not get beaten by the son of his. At the end Philip was triumphant and the outcome of the fight was to make his authority supreme and supreme over all countries of Greece.

Alexander's Impetuosity. Philip Rejects Olympias - Despite however, the remarkable intelligence and discretion that characterized Alexander's mind Alexander during his beginning times, he was frequently aggressive and arrogant and, in instances where his pride or his anger were in the air the man was often found to be extremely impetuous and uncontrollable. The mother of his son Olympias was a woman of a brazen and flamboyant temper and she argued with her husband Philip, the king. Philip Perhaps it is better to be said that he fought with her. The two are believed as having been infidelity one another, and following a fierce dispute, Philip repudiated his wife and got married to another woman. In the celebrations that were celebrated to mark the marriage was a huge banquet in which Alexander was also present. During the event, an incident took place that shows the recklessness that his nature.

Alexander's Violent Temper. of the guests who attended the banquet when he made a comment of praise to the queen's new heir was able to use expressions that Alexander thought were a mockery of the persona of his mother as well as himself. His fury was instantly ignited. He threw the drink the one he was drinking into the head of the offender. Attalus because that was the name he used, toss his drink at Alexander and returned the favor. The people at the table they were seated rose, and a scene of rage as well as confusion ensued.

Philip's Strike on his Son Philip angry at an infraction to the peace and order of the wedding celebration was furious and drew his sword. He ran towards Alexander however, due to an accident the sailor fell and slid to the floor. Alexander was shocked and looked at his dead father with a look of disdain and contempt and exclaimed "What an excellent hero do the nations of Greece must have in their armies. He is the only one who can traverse the floor without falling." Then he disengaged from the royal palace and left. Afterward, he joined with his mother Olympias and left with her to her home homeland, Epirus, where the mother and son were for a while in a state of public dispute with their husband and father.

Philip's Power. His plans of conquer - In the meantime, Philip had begun organizing a major expedition into Asia. He had orchestrated all the business of his kingdom, and had also arranged an effective alliance among all the nations of Greece with the aim of establishing powerful armies were raised and he was commissioned to be their commander. His mind was fully engaged in this huge undertaking. He was in the midst of his life and was at the peak of his influence. His kingdom was in the best of health and prosperity condition, and his superiority over the other kingdoms as well as countries in the

European side was fully established. He was full of determination and optimism. He was happy for his son Alexander and was counting on his assistance in his plans of conquer and advancement. He had gotten married to a young beautiful bride and was in a throng of celebrations as well as rejoicing and celebration. He was anticipating an extremely successful career, based on all the good deeds have been accomplished and the fame he gained as a mere introduction as a prelude for the more prestigious and prominent role that he planned to play.

Alexander's Insatiableness to Reign Alexander in the midst of time, passionate and impetuous and aspired to glory as he was at the status and future that his grandfather had enjoyed with jealousy and envy. He was eager to become a the monarch of his own. The reason he sided so swiftly to his wife in the family dispute was in part due to the belief the father of his was an hindrance and hindrance in path to his own glory and fame. He felt that within him were the powers and capabilities that allowed him to assume the place of his father and reap the fruits of glory and power that seemed to be waiting for the

Grecian army in the upcoming campaign. As long as his father lived but he was able to be a prince, powerful well-educated, popular, and successful however but without powerful and independent authority. He was uneasy and restless with the thought that because his father was in the peak of his energy and vitality manhood, long periods of time would pass before he would escape this imprisoned and subordinate position. The restlessness and anxiety of his werehowever abruptly resolved by an incredibly bizarre event that prompted him, in a mere hour's notice, to assume his father's place on the throne.

Chapter 3: The Beginning Of His Reign

B.C. 336

Alexander was unexpectedly called upon to succeed his father to the Macedonian throne in the most surprising manner, and amid scenes of great tension and excitement. The reasons were:

Philip is at peace with Olympias and Alexander Philip has been reconciled with Alexander and Olympias. Philip was extremely enthralled prior to embarking on his grand expedition to Asia to be reconciled with Alexander as well as Olympias. Philip wished Alexander's support in his plans. And in addition the risk, it was dangerous to leave his own responsibilities with an unrequited son, with a sense of resentment and hatred.

Olympias as well as Alexander returned. Philip wrote conciliatory and friendly notes towards Olympias and Alexander who had left, they will be remembered, to Epirus where her friends resided. Alexander's brother Olympias was the King of Epirus. He was initially angered by the injustice that was imposed on his sister because of Philip's treatment however Philip was now trying to ease his anger through friendly negotiations and messages. Finally, he organized for a wedding between this Emperor of Epirus and one of his daughters, and that was the end of the reconciliation. Olympias along with Alexander went back to Macedon and impressive preparations were put into place for a stunning wedding.

The grand wedding was a great celebration. Philip was determined to make the wedding more than only a way of confirming the reconciliation he had with his ex-wife and son, but also for establishing good relations towards the King of Epirus He also saw the occasion as an opportunity for paying attention with a high-quality and respectful manner towards the princes as well as generals from the different states in Greece. Therefore, he prepared his celebrations in a large and extravagant size, and made invitations to powerful and notable men from all over the world and even closer.

The great men however as well as all other officials of the different Grecian states, sent congratulations as well as congratulations and gifts to Philip and his family, each one seeming determined to be a part of the joy of the celebration. They weren't completely uninterested in this, and it's evident. Since Philip was appointed commander-in-chief of the Grecian armies that were set to conquer Asia and as the king's influence and power in everything associated with this huge undertaking would be supreme and absolute; and also because everyone wanted to be a part in the glory of this expeditionand also to share in the greatest extent possible with the power and fame that seemed to be at the disposal of Philip, everyone were eager to win his favour. Just a few days earlier they began to fight against him, but after he had gained his position as the leader, everyone was eager to join to work towards enhancing the glory of his reign and making it famous.

Planning for the Wedding. Expensive presents - And neither could Philip be content with the insincerity and hollowness of these declarations of friendship. The praises and favors Philip offered them were also heartless and hollow. He wanted to win their approval as a way to assist him on the mountain of fame and glory that was his aim to climb. They wanted his to ensure that he could climb himself and to help them climb by helping them up. It was the most charming display of affectionate and loyal friendship. Cities sent him gifts with golden crowns that were beautifully designed and made of premium price. Other embassies sent letters to express their sincere wishes for the man, and their trust in the accomplishment in his ideas. Athens The city that was the center of science and literature in Greece wrote a poem in which the tale of the expedition to Persia was told through anticipation. In the poetry Philip was, obviously the most triumphantly successful of his mission. He led his army safely through the most treacherous passages and defiles, was a champion in battle, earned impressive victories, and was able to avail himself of the wealth of Asiatic power and wealth. It should be noted but in fairness to the poet when he narrates his fictitious adventures, he was able to portray Philip as well as the Persian ruler with fictional names.

The celebration of the Wedding. Games and Spectacles The wedding was held at one city in Macedon with great spectacle and pomp. The celebrations included games spectacles, as well as civic and military spectacles of every kind to entertain the thousands viewers who gathered to watch these events. One of these shows they held a parade of gods' statues. There were twelve statues, all sculpted with great artistic skill, and carried along on pedestals elevated along with censers and incense, as well as various rituals of homage. Huge crowds of people walked along the route. There was a 13th statue that was more impressive than the others, that represented Philip himself as the persona of a god.

Gods and Statues Gods It was not at all immoral as it may initially appear to be, since the gods that the ancients revered were in actuality, deifications of the kings and heroes of old who lived in the early time and earned the reputation of having supernatural powers due to their famed actions, which were exaggerated according to the customs of the time in superstitious times. The masses of ignorant people at the time revered the king of the present with the same respect and reverence as they did their idols who were deified. They provided them with the same ideas of God. The idea of making a monarch god was, therefore, not a very lavish flattery.

Military Procession - As the procession of statues with the troopers with trumpets blaring with banners fluttering. The officers rode horses that were elegantly caparisoned and dancing in awe. They escorted princes generals, embassadors and other great state officers and were all stunningly dressed in their formal attire, wearing badges and insignia.

The appearance of Philip - Finally, the King Philip himself was seen during the parade. Philip had planned to have a huge space left, which was in his middle he had to take a walk. This was done so as to make his place most prominent and to emphasize his high standing over the other kings that were in attendance at the event. Guards were able to follow him, although at a some distance, as it was already mentioned. He was robed in white robes and his head was decorated with a beautiful crown.

The Scene changed. The assassination of Philip The procession was heading towards the great theater in which certain spectacles and games were scheduled to be displayed. The gods' statues were to be carried to the theater, and then placed in prominent positions within the sight of the crowd before the procession was scheduled to be followed. The statues were all in with the exception of Philip who was right in front of the entrance, and Philip himself was moving through the area left along the avenue through the entrance to the theater and a momentous event occurred, in which all the nature of the scene as well as the fate of Alexander and the fate of fifty nations was abruptly and completely altered. The reason was this. A guardsman in his place at the front of the procession, right next to the king, was observed speeding towards him across the distance that was separating him from the others and, before people could even think about what he was going be doing, he cut him in the heart. Philip fell to the street and perished.

An unimaginable scene of tumult and confusion followed. The perpetrator was immediately taken away by other guards. They discovered, however, just before his death that it was Pausanias who was a man with a high status and influence and a general officer of the guards. He was provided with horses and other help available to help him escape, however his life was taken away by the guards before he was able to use them.

Alexander proclaimed King. Alexander's Speech - A state official of the state immediately rushed to Alexander and declared to Alexander the death of his father and his ascendance to the throne. A gathering of the most powerful leaders and statemen was called in a chaotic and fast-paced manner and Alexander was proclaimed King with massive and general applause. Alexander delivered a speech in the rebuttal. The large crowd was captivated by his young face and form when he stood up and listened with awe-inspiring curiosity to see what he had speak. He was between the ages of nineteen and twenty-two years old; however even though he was young but he spoke with the determination and confidence of a spirited man. He told me that he must immediately take over his father's place and carry on his plans. He was hoping to accomplish it so effectively that the entire process could be carried out exactly as the case had been if his father continued to live and the entire nation would discover it was only a change that took place was by the name of the King.

Demosthenes' Philippics - The motivation behind Pausanias' decision to kill Philip in the manner he did was never determined. There were a variety of opinions on the murder. The most popular was that it was a private act of revenge that was triggered by a mistake or injury Pausanias received from Philip. Some believed that the killing was the result of a faction within those states in Greece which were opposed towards Philip and were unable to accept to let him command forces of the allied armies, which were about to enter Asia. Demosthenes was a famous actor, became Philip's greatest antagonist in the ranks of Greeks. The most effective orations were designed to arouse his fellow citizens to oppose his ambitious plans and limit his influence. The speeches were referred to as his Philippics and from their source has come the practice that has remained in place since then of using the term philippics to refer to generally any harshly denunciatory harangue.

The Greeks were suspected of being the perpetrators - Today Demosthenes is reported to have that he was at the time in Athens was the one who declared his death Philip at an Athenian gathering prior to when it was believed that the information could have been communicated to them. He justified his early knowledge of the information by saying that it was sent to him by a few of gods. Many people believe that the plot to kill Philip was thought up in Greece and that Demosthenes was part of it, and they believe that Pausanias was the one responsible in executing it And that Demosthenes was so sure of the outcome of the plot and so euphoric in the certainty of this plan, that he was unable to resist the urge of anticipating the announcement.

The Persians also had other people who believed that Persians had planned and carried out this crime, provoking Pausanias into committing the crime through the promise of large rewards. Because Pausanias himself was instantly killed so there was no possibility of getting any information from him about the motives behind his actions or even if he might be inclined to share any information.

Alexander's new role was, in all likelihood, Alexander found himself suddenly elevated to one of the most prominent post in the world of politics. It wasn't simply because Alexander was crowned the king of Macedon and even this could have been an impressive post for a young man, but Macedon was only a tiny portion of the kingdom over which Philip was extending his authority. The authority he achieved over the entire Grecian empire, as well as the extensive arrangements he constructed for an expansion into Asia and beyond, led to Alexander the subject of worldwide fascination and interest. The issue was whether Alexander should try to assume his father's role in regard to this power, and continue and implement his huge plans, or if he should settle for a quiet reign quietly over his Macedonia. Macedon.

His Plans - The most prudent individuals would advise a prince of the age of 18 in such circumstances to take the second option. However, Alexander did not have any idea of limiting his ambition to any of these limitations. He was determined to leap instantly into the seat of his father and not just be the holder of all of the authority that his father was able to acquire, but also to immediately begin the most vigorous and energetic efforts to extend the reach of it.

Murderers of Philip Penalized - His primary strategy was to bring down the murderers of his father. He caused the events of the incident to be examined, as well as those who were believed to have been associated to Pausanias as part of the conspiracy were brought before a judge. Though the motives and plans of the perpetrators could not be determined, certain people had been found guilty for having been involved in the plot and sentenced to be executed in public.

Alexander's first acts Alexander then decided to not alter his father's appointment to the state's most important offices however, he decided to let the entire department of public affairs continue with the same people like they had been before. What a shrewd line of conduct! Young and passionate men, under the situation where he was were likely to have been thrilled and astonished at their rise and would replace the older and well-trained servants of the father with their personal favorite from their own generation untrained and incompetent and just as arrogant as they were. Alexander nevertheless made no modifications. Alexander continued to have the same officers in charge, attempting to ensure that everything ran exactly as the way it would have been if his father hadn't passed away.

Parmenio Two officers specifically who were ministers upon whom Philip had mostly relied. The names of these officers included Antipater as well as Parmenio. Antipater was in charge of the civil and Parmenio was the military's chief. Parmenio was a distinguished general. He was close to sixty years old. Alexander believed in his military skills and had a strong personal bond with his fellow soldiers. Parmenio was drafted into the service of the young king with excellent readiness and was with throughout the entirety of his time. It was strange to observe men of that years of standing, age and seasoned, observing the instructions of young men. But there was something about the wit, the strength and the passion of Alexander's character that inspired passion in the people who were around him. He caused everyone to follow his lead and assist in the implementation of his plans.

Cities from Southern Greece. Athens and Corinth Athens and Corinth Macedon As shown on the map below is located in the northern region of the country that was occupied by the Greeks and was one of one of the strongest states of the confederacy as well as all the major and powerful cities were situated south of it. There was Athens that was magnificently constructed, its impressive citadel crowned by a rock hill that was situated in the middle of the. It was the capital city in the fields of philosophy, literature and the arts which made it a major point of interest for all of the civilized world. There was Corinth and it was noted by the glitz and fun that was prevalent there. Every possible avenue of entertainment and luxury were abound within the walls. The seekers of knowledge and art from all over the globe, came to Athens and those seeking enjoyment, relaxation and indulgence chose Corinth as their place of residence. Corinth was an idyllic spot in the isthmus, and had views of the ocean on either side. Corinth was a renowned city for more than a thousand years during Alexander's time.

The map of Macedon and Greece

Thebes Also, there was Thebes. Thebes was further from the north of Athens or Corinth. It was located on an elevated plain and was, like many other cities of the past it had a strong citadel which was also at the time an Macedonian garrison that Philip was able to establish there. Thebes was extremely wealthy and strong. It was also celebrated as the birthplace of numerous philosophers and poets, as well as other notable men. One of them were Pindar an extremely renowned poet who flourished just around two centuries before the reign of Alexander. His descendants were still living in Thebes and Alexander was later on, perhaps after occurred, was able to confer on them an extremely prestigious honor.

Sparta The city was Sparta and it was also known as Lacedaemon. The residents of this city were famous for their strength, courage and physical strength as well as for the vigor with which they dedicated themselves to the task of the war. They were almost all soldiers. The structures of the state, of society, as well as the plans for education were designed to foster an attitude of military pride and ambition in the officers as well as ferocious and unstoppable endurance and courage in men.

Conquests of Philip The cities of these as well as many others, along as well as the states connected to them, formed an enormous, flourishing extremely powerful and well-organized community that spanned the part of Greece that was to the south of Macedon. Philip was, as it has been previously mentioned, established his own authority over the entire region even though it took numerous tense negotiations and difficult battles to achieve it. Alexander was unsure that the citizens of cities and states were willing to hand over easily, especially to such a young an heir to the throne as he was, the high commission that was his grandfather, who had been a strong monarch and soldier was able to extort from them with such trouble. What was the best course of action in this case? Should he renounce the idea of it? Should he approach embassadors them, and present his claim to take over his father's position? Or should he decide not to act in any way, and instead sit at home quietly at home in Macedon until they make a decision?

Alexander is marching south - In lieu of undertaking either of these, Alexander decided on the very bold move of setting himself as the leader of an entire army to make his way through the southern part of Greece to the point of presenting himself in person and, if required in proving claims to the exact position of honor and authority that was bestowed to his father. Given the facts of the situation this may have been one of the most bold and most determined actions of Alexander's entire career. A number of his Macedonian advisors advised him against the same move, However, Alexander was not going to listen to any advice from them. Alexander assembled his army and marched off at the top of them.

Pass of Thermopylae between Macedon as well as the states in southern Greece was a series of high and nearly impassable mountains. They spanned the entire interior of Greece, and the main road leading to the southern part of Greece traversed to the east of them. There, they were capped by cliffs. They left an in-between passage between the cliffs as well as the sea. This pass was known as The Pass of Thermopylae and was thought to be as the main entrance point to Greece. It was also a city dubbed Anthela close to the pass located on the outside.

It was the Amphictyonic Council - There was at that time a type of general assembly or congress for the different states of Greece that would be held periodically time to settle issues and disagreements that the various states were always involved with one another. This gathering was known as "the Amphictyonic Council, on account of the fact of being founded in the name of a certain monarch called Amphictyon. The council was set up to receive Alexander. The event was to take place at Thermopylae or, more accurately it was at Anthela The latter was without the pass and was also the typical spot where the council would meet. The reason for this was that the pass was located in an intermediate location between the northern and southern regions of Greece and was therefore accessible from both.

It was March that passed through Thessaly. Alexander's character traits - When he was moving to the south, Alexander had first to travel through Thessaly which was a powerful state just to the south of Macedon. Alexander was met with a bit of resistance in the beginning but it was not too much. The nation was impressed by the determination and courage of character exhibited by the decision to take such an arduous course for such an individual. Also, Alexander, so far as he was known personally as a person, left a very positive impression on all. His athletic and masculine appearance as well as his open and honest manners, his spirit his kindness and an air of self-confidence, independence and a sense of superiority that were all melded with a sense of self-confidence and independence, which is always the case in the context of genuine excellence, with an unaffected and unassuming self-confidence - these and many other qualities, which were apparent to everyone who met his persona and personality of Alexander who made everybody his best friend. People of all ages enjoy being influenced by and power of someone whom they perceive and believe is of a greater level and has more power that their own. They are drawn to the leader. They should be confident about his superiority, but only when that superiority is clearly and clearly as well as mingled with the graces and appeals of youth and beauty, such as with the example of Alexander and his followers, the minds of people are quickly and effortlessly into its grip.

The Thessalians are joined by Alexander The Thessalians join Alexander The They gave Alexander an extremely warm welcome. They expressed their readiness to reinstate Alexander in the post that his father was occupying. They joined their forces with his and sped to the south, towards The Pass in Thermopylae.

He is a member of the Amphictyonic council - This is where the council of great importance was held. Alexander was elected to it as an individual member. Of course, he should be the subject of all-encompassing attention and interest. The impression he left in this instance appears to have been extremely positive. Following the dissolution of this assembly, Alexander proceeded southward, with his own troops and was accompanied by numerous princes and potentates of Greece along with their companions and followers. The exuberant feelings and delight that the young king walked across The Pass of Thermopylae, thus were exhilarating to say the least.

Thermopylae. Leonidas as well as the Spartans - - The Pass of Thermopylae is an epic scene that is strongly associated with concepts of prestige and military glory. It was in this area that just a few 100 and 50 years earlier, Leonidas, a Spartan general with just three hundred troops was attempting to stand up to the immense Persian force at the moment attacking Greece. The general was among the Kings of Sparta and had the authority, not only of his 3 hundred Spartans however, but also of all the forces of the Greeks who were gathered to fight off from the Persian invasion. With the assistance of his allies, he fought his Persian forces for a while and, as the pass was thin between the cliffs as well as the ocean, he was capable of defeating them. However, at the end an enthralling detachment of the massive Persian army managed to make their way across the mountains and into the pass, in order to put themselves in a position from where they could fall on the tiny Greek army to their rear. Leonidas realizing this, instructed the allies of various states within Greece to leave to leave him as well as his 300 countrymen on their own within the darkness.

Died of Leonidas. Spartan courage He didn't expect to fend off his enemies, or fight for the passage. He was aware that he would go to the grave, with his faithful followers and that the stream of invaders would pour down the pass and over their bodies. However, he believed that he was there to protect the pass and would not leave his position. As the battle began, it was he who was first to be killed. The soldiers were gathered around him, and they defended the body of his deceased to the extent they could. In the end, beaten by the massive number of their adversaries the soldiers were killed all with the exception of one. He fled back to Sparta. A monument was built at the site with the message: "Go, traveler, to Sparta and declare that we are here on the site where the troops were deployed to protect our nation."

Alexander made commander-in-chief. He then returned to Macedon as commander-in-chief. Alexander went by the defile. He travelled to the major cities to its south, including Athens and then to Thebes and finally to Corinth. A great gathering of all the kings and potentates of Greece was held in Corinth and it was here that Alexander reached the goal of his ambitions, by being given the command of the massive expedition into Asia granted to Alexander. The impression that he made on those who he had come to be associated through his character and qualities would be favorable to the greatest extent. The fact that a prince of his age was chosen by such a powerful a group of nations to be their leader in an undertaking as they planned to take part in, demonstrates an remarkable power on his behalf of ascending over the minds of people, and also of enthralling everyone with a sense of dominance. Alexander was returned to Macedon after his trip to the south in victory, and set off promptly to arrange the administration of his kingdom so that he could be prepared to set out, without hesitation on the grand adventure of conquer that he envisioned was ahead of him.

Chapter 4: Battle Of Persia

The map prior to the Alexander's conquest. Courtesy of the University of Florida

In 334 when Alexander began his war against Persia and conquer Persia, the area covered nearly the entire the world to the east Macedon the present day Turkey, Syria, Lebanon, Jordan, Israel, Egypt, Iraq, Kuwait, Iran and Afghanistan. It was extremely wealthy and powerful, but not without problems.

According to Xenephon an mercenary who engaged during the war in Persia sixty years prior to the war "it was obvious to anyone paying close focus on the dimensions of the kingdom of the king that it was powerful in terms of land and people, but fragile due to the vast distances of roads and the dispersal of its troops in the event of a conduct a quick strike at it."

This signified it was that Persian Empire was huge but heavy structure, that could be seized by a strong army, and that offered the possibility of an increase in the wealth of conquerors, an empire that was to be sought-after instead of to be feared.

The Greeks did not ignore the Persian invasion of the 5th century in the beginning. Although they lost that famous war of Marathon in 490 BC, they fought back under the leadership of Xerxes with a huge army, destroying those Spartans in the legendary Battle of Thermopylae (the basis of the film 300) and then capturing and demolish the majority of Athens. In the end, the Persians were exiled, but the Greeks did not forget what they had done and were determined to get their revenge.

March to Persia

Battle of Granicus River. Battle of Granicus River

Alexander conquered the Hellespont in the spring of 334BC, accompanied by roughly 32,000 soldiers (12,000 Macedonian hoplites, 12,000 Greek archers and infantrymen) along with 5,100 soldiers (1,800 Macedonian heavy cavalry and the rest of the Greeks).

He was the pilot during the Hellespont crossing in order to duplicate the feat that the heroic Protesilaus and was the first to land on shore.

Alexander was spear-wielding and declared Asia was" the land that was won by spears." He swung into Troy and, as the new Achilles made his war a tribute to Athena. He declared that the whole of Asia was to be conquered through his spear. Macedonian spear.

When Alexander traveled to Asia Alexander had only seventy talents worth of gold, and barely enough food to last for a month. He knew he had to fight quickly, but first, he needed to please the gods in order to honor the Greek heroes who traversed through the Hellespont earlier than him. He took a deliberate excursion to the location that was Ancient Troy, sacrificing at the grave of Achilles (Alexander's hero) and his most trusted friend Hephaestion was sacrificed at the burial site of Patroclus, Achilles closest friend. Alexander also offered sacrifice in The temple of Athena and deposited the robes of Armour. In exchange , he took away his "sacred shield Athena," which was believed to have been left in the temple in the Trojan war, which made it about 880 years old. The shield would have been taken to the Macedonian hoplites, and is believed to have saved Alexander's life his hometown of Mallians during his period in India.

With no food or pay to last for four weeks Alexander knew he had to act quickly in order to get the Persians to the battlefield and collect some war spoils to pay his soldiers. Persian Darius III, the Persian King Darius III obviously didn't feel to be threatened by Alexander decided to leave the defense up to the local Satraps (governors) and decided instead of advancing to cut off Alexander immediately, to keep the line along the Grancicus River, in Mysia.

The Battle of the Granicus River was the first of three major battles fought by Alexander the Great and the Persian Empire. Near the location of Troy the battle occurred within Northwestern Asia Minor. Alexander was successful in defeating the forces of the Persian Satraps who were from Asia Minor which included a massive force of Greek mercenaries led Memnon from Rhodes. Satrap: Satrap was the title that was that was given to the governors of provinces in the old Persian Empire.

Arrian of Nicodemia composed a number of narratives about the battle. Arrian was Greek historian public service, commander of the military, and philosopher.

Below is a description of the way Alexander strategically created his army:

"Alexander was sent Parmenio to assume control of the left wing while the rest of his men towards the left. He already had on the line a few commanders. To the left was Philotas, the son of Parmenio who was who was in charge of the cavalry of companions along with the archers as well as the Agrianian javelinmen and next to him was Amyntas, the son of Arrabaeus who was responsible for the lancers as well as his fellow Paeonians along with the team of Socrates following were the royal guards under the command of Nicanor who was the son of Parmenio then they were the phalanx under the leadership of Perdiccas, son of Orontes in the next group, and after them, the troops led by Coenus who was the son of Polemocrates as well as those commanded by Amyntas who was the son of Andromenes as well as on the right side, the phalanx of Philip the his son from Amyntas. On the left side and the Thessalian cavalry first appeared under the command of Calas, the son of Harpalus in the middle, and behind them were the allied cavalry under the command of Philip who was his son from Menelaus as well as Agatho was the commander of the Thracian group. Beyond them were infantry battalions, including the phalanx of Craterus and the phalanx of Craterus, followed by those that of Meleager and Philip until in the middle of fighting line."

The Persians expanded through Zelea to the close Granicus River. The Granicus River is between 60 and 90 feet in width. Due to its different levels of depth, powerful currents, and steep banks , this could create an obstacle to Alexander's cavalry. It would also make it difficult for his phalanxes to maintain their position. The Persians established a strong defensive position on the eastern bank and placed all their cavalry in the front line, creating as wide a front as possible-- approximately 7,500 feet, or 1.4 miles. They believed that they could be able to take on enemies with javelins that were thrown from an elevated position, they waited with awe to see the coming that of their Macedonian army. They also had a huge group of Greek mercenaries who were in reserve.

The Battle of the Graniccus began with the Persian leaders were focused on the movement of Alexander in their determination to take him down. Alexander became a noticeable target because of the shimmering armor he was wearing and the white plumes that hung from his helmet.

The Persians were able to see Alexander as the leader of the cavalry on their right side, and believed that he was planning to strike them from their left. The Persians moved several regiments of their cavalry from their central position and placed over and on the riverbanks to the right of Alexander who they expected to launch his main assault.

The tension was apparent, the two sides fighting in silence. Alexander initiated the battle with a forward-moving force. A total of 950 horses and an army of infantry (1.000 soldiers) launched a flimsy attack on Persia's most left flank, with Socrates The squadron led the approach.

Arrian who's report on the war is most thorough and reliable, had this to write "'At the point at which Amyntas's vanguard as well as Socrates crossed the river at the point where the Persians fired volleys at the above from above, with others throwing their javelins over the stream from the post along the river's bank. while others heading down to the river on more level ground. There was a lot of cavalry shoving in the course of trying to escape the river, while others tried were trying to block them. massive waves of Persian javelins, and a lot of throwing into the river, and a lot of thrusting Macedonian spears. However, the Macedonians were a lot outnumbered and suffered a terrible loss in the initial attack as they defended themselves from the river, on ground that was not solid and was under the enemy's while the Persians were able to take advantage of the bank. In particular flowers of Persian cavalry was stationed there, and Memnon's sons as well as Memnon himself fought alongside them. They were the first Macedonians who were able to come to terms to the Persians were slain regardless of their courage.'

Although Macedonian advance forces were weak, and the Macedonian forces in advance were insufficient and was met with fierce resistance and heavy losses, it was successful in pulling its Persian Left flank cavalry from their lines. After that, Alexander's trumpets began blaring commands, before launching his primary attack. He led his cavalry, which was the elite of the army, to the front. They fought to the east bank as the Persians fired javelins at them.

Arrian explained the fighting at the time. "though the fighting took place on horses, it was more of an infantry fight in which horses were entangled with horses and man against man in the battle and it was the Macedonians trying to force the Persians one and for all off the bank and bring them onto the level ground, and the Persians trying to block their landing, and then hurling them back into the river.'

While the feint attack was in progress, Alexander along with the other members of the troops were moving forward, battle cries sounding as they crossed the river.

The Persian leaders realized Alexander the Persian leader, they rode out to confront him in hand-to-hand combat. The lance of Alexander (sarissa) was splintered in his first fight and he demanded a new one. As he waited, he courageously engaged his adversaries. The fight was currently the forward point. The moment he got his first victory, he

Another sarissa, a Persian cavalry commander called Mithridates was seen at the top of an entire squadron. Alexander was riding forward when he struck him on the face with his sarissa , killing the man instantly. Another Persian nobleman known as Rhoesaces came into the scene with his scimitar, and cut off a part of Alexander's head, leaving small wounds.

Cleitus Commander of the Royal Squadron, who was given the task of keeping the king safe , anticipated the attack and cut off his Persians sword arm, saving Alexander's life.

The Macedonians were constantly coming along the banks, and the Persians tried to keep them back into the river. They wanted to prevent the Macedonians from gaining an edging and then rushing across the banks. Arrian wrote:" He wrote, "The Persians were being treated from all sides They as well as their horses were hit in the face by lances and sarissasand were pulled back by the Companioncavalry, and in a lot of pain from the light troops which had joined together with Cavalry.' "

The Macedonians slowly, but surely, took the Persians further back, eventually gaining the ground level over the river's bank. In the wake of the departure of many of its leaders , the Persian cavalry was beginning to decline. The first unit to break down to the Persian line in which Alexander was fighting. The entire center fell apart. After the center collapsed, two wings of Persian cavalry flew away in panic. The Macedonian army was unable to chase the cavalry that fled due to the fact that they were surrounded by the Persian Greek mercenary infantry was in the middle of their territory, blocking Alexander's route.

The mercenary group gave Alexander the conditions under which they could surrender, however Alexander refused and, wanting to show his respect for those who were "traitors" the soldiers were killed, with only 2,000 out of 20,000 killed in the battle and sold to slavery in Greece. Alexander was the one to command all who were killed during the Battle of Granicus, including Persian leaders as well as Greek the mercenaries, to be laid to rest with honors of the military.

Alexander's courageous leadership of being in battle at the center of battle and just barely escaping death was rewarded by Diodorus with the "palm for courage" and also gave him his first major victory against the Persians and opened the way to the western and southern parts of Asia Minor. After the victory at Granicus the Greek cities in Asia Minor were liberated from Persian control and the beachhead was reserving for future campaigns further into Persian territories.

Chapter 5: Moving Forward To Issus

Following the Battle of Granicus River Alexander was in a position to take control of Asia Minor. Without threat of attack, Alexander was in a position to return to Macedonia to winterize any males who were married prior to the start of the campaign. This had the double benefit of increasing Alexander's number within his army, as well as in boosting that of the army, as they purchased new recruits.

Alexander was able to secure his supply lines, and did something unprecedented in the past.

the campaign continued through the winter. This allowed Alexander to protect the western and southern coasts from Asia Minor, which meant that the Persians were unable to put their ships in and then attack Alexander from behind.

In the spring of 333BC, Alexander was preparing to meet with his soldiers who had returned and new recruits in Gordium situated which is located in the middle of Turkey. In Gordium, he toured the famous oxcart that was a part of King Gordium. The oxen's yoke was connected to a pole that was so intricate that it was difficult to remove. Legend has it that the one who could untie this Gordian knot would be the king of Asia. Alexander attempted to tie the knot but could not. In order to fulfill the prophecy Alexander used his blade and cut through the knot. Alexander declared that the prophecy had been fulfilled. He also stated that there were no limits to the ways knots could be cut. Although he may have cheated, it was a great publicity.

Following Gordium Alexander went on to advance throughout Asia Minor unchallenged to the Cilician gates, which was a narrow passage that could be quickly defended. The Persian defenses, however, fled as Alexander came closer, leaving Macedonians free to move through and take over the wealthy cities of Tarsus and to open the coastline, which is now modern Israel as well as Lebanon.

When he reached Tarsus Alexander had taken a dip in the frigid waters in the Cydnus River after a long journey and was struck by fever. It took Alexander 2 months for recovery from.

Following the loss at Granicus After the defeat at Granicus, River Darius assumed the personal charge over his Persian army. Darius had gathered a huge army in Sochi Modern Syria and, upon hearing this news, Alexander was sent south to confront the entire force of Persian army.

Alexander took most of his wounded and sick soldiers and heavy equipment for siege at Issus in the hope of taking Darius to the battle. After two days, Alexander realized that he committed a grave error. When he was heading to the south along the western side of the mountains close to shore, Darius had travelled north along the eastern side, and then moved in front of Alexander and cut off Alexander's supply lines, causing Alexander either to fight for his life or die. Alexander was forced to fight or starve. Persians were also able to kill and tortured the wounded and sick in Issus.

The Persians with their larger army, sat down at the North bank of the Penarus River, near Issus and were waiting for Alexander to change his mind and counter-marsh back in order to meet the Persians. It was a chilly and wet day on November 5th 333BC , when both armies confronted each one another along the River. There were plenty of boulders along the river, which meant that horses charged with a heavy load were in danger of breaking their legs. The banks at times would become difficult to scale.

The situation facing Alexander wasn't as bad as it looked, the Persians were able to draw up an extremely narrow coastal plain just two miles wide which had the ocean on one side while mountains to the opposite. This means that Darius did not have enough space to accommodate all Persian troops, whereas Alexander was able to completely be able to deploy his.

Darius was able to benefit from the advantages of being the first to arrive at the site of the battle initially set his cavalry army of 30,000 and 90,000 infantry to the northern side of the river. He positioned his troops in a large block in the middle, with the majority of his cavalry on his right side close to the ocean. There was also a part of his army in the hills to the left. Darius himself was at the middle with his cavalry guards. They were in the back of the Greek Mercenaries.

Alexander was on the other hand was a smaller army comprising 5,300 cavalry as well as 24,000 infantry. He placed his own position on the left of his infantry along with the Macedonian cavalry, while Parmenio was in charge of his Thessaly along with the Allied cavalry on his left.

The battle began with the Alexander's signature movements. Alexander charged using his Companion cavalry to the right, crossing the river in the speed of a charge, and then in the process, he broke through Persian resistance. Darius was also fighting the Persian resistance. Darius engaged The Thessaly cavalry to his left however due to the restricted space available, was not able to deploy his vast number of troops. Despite the pressure of pushing Parmenio as well as his Thessaly cavalry back, they could not break through.

Remaining on the right side, Alexander's charge had penetrated his Persian Infantry Line. To his left, the remainder of the cavalry crossed the river , engaging and then repressing the Persians. The whole left wing to fall and take a different route. Alexander turned towards the center, threatening the Greek mercenaries that were surrounding Darius. Darius after noticing that his line was breached, turned around and left the fight.

Alexander instead of running after Darius moved to in the direction of Darius, he stayed behind the Persian line to help Parmenio. The escape of Darius led to the morale to fall and, at the risk of being attacked, the Persian cavalry began to flee. Because of the huge quantity of soldiers they ended up within range of each other and Alexander was able to win the victory. Despite his efforts to chase Darius into mountain ranges Alexander was unsuccessful in capturing Darius who was later able to regroup to continue.

Alexander was able capture the Persian camp, which included 3000 talent made up of Gold in silver and Gold, Darius his wife, mother, and two daughters. They were held hostage, and treated with respect as was expected of royal family. Darius informed them they were alive. Darius still existed. Darius would attempt to swap Darius for half his kingdom but Alexander refused.

The next day Alexander was to officiate at a funeral for all the Persian, Macedonian and Greek soldiers who were killed on Issus and would also visit the wounded during their recovery.

Chapter 6: The Siege Of Tyre

After the triumph in Issus, Alexander had the option of continuing his march towards the east and towards Persia to search for Darius before he could recoup and finance another Army or to move south towards the Mediterranean coast to eliminate his Persians naval power. Alexander picked the latter option.

In this time, the strength of your navy relied on the strength of the ports, as Ancient ships were unable to be able to operate from land, nor could they be in the sea for an extended duration as they carried only a small amount of water or food.

Alexander was a soldier who led his army down the coast of Phoenicia with an army of 35,000 to 4000 strong. The cities in the north quickly surrendered and accept Alexander to be their new lord. Alexander was crowned the new king from Byblus along with Sidon. Tyrian representatives contacted Alexander as he was in an unofficial march and declared that they were going to respect his wishes.

Alexander's dream was simple. He wanted to sacrifice himself for Heracles within Tyre. The

Tyrians believed this might be a plot by Alexander to gain access and take over the city. Alexander declined, however, they did state that Alexander was free to sacrifice for Heracles within Old Tyre, which was constructed on the mainland , and had no strategic significance. It was just the King of Tyre who could make sacrifices in the name of Heracles at The Main Temple in New Tyre and in doing so Alexander could be trying to establish himself as King. The Tyrians did not agree and closed their harbor and gates in the direction of the Macedonians.

The Tyrian's refusal was akin to declaring war on Alexander.

Tyrians Tyrians knew of Alexander's rising fame but they were confident as they had a mighty army of mercenaries and navy. Their city was situated about one mile offshore and, according to Arrian the walls on the landward-facing side soared to a staggering 150 feet. in size. Its defences Tyre were strong and had fought off a variety of besiegers during the time. They Tyrians began to move the majority of their children and women to their colony in Carthage leaving behind approximately 40000 people. Carthage has also promised to provide military assistance including boats and even soldiers.

Alexander recognized that Tyre was believed to be impregnable. He therefore called a war council. He informed his generals of that it was crucial to protect the entire Phoenician cities prior to advancing into Egypt. Tyre is a stronghold of the Persian fleet, and leaving them there would be a threat to Alexander's rear. In the hope of avoiding the long and arduous siege, as a final effort, Alexander sent heralds to Tyre asking them to surrender, however, the heralds were killed and their bodies dumped into the ocean.

Alexander began his work following the failure of negotiations in the month of January, 332 BC. Alexander retreated to the old Tyre and then began building an causeway (or mole) across the channel towards the wall of Tyre with the help of wood, rocks and rubble he gathered from the structures of the city's old. The work began well, but the water close to the shoreline was relatively shallow however as the causeway became larger, the Macedonians and Greeks started to encounter difficulties. The depth of the sea was growing to 18 feet. The pace of work slowed down, and the gangs of workers found themselves being snatched by missiles coming from within the walls of city.

Alexander built two towers of siege and placed them on the other side of the causeway. The artillery engines on high up in the towers could shoot back at the walls. Alexander was known to spend a lot of his time in the mole. He also distributed tiny amounts of money to his workers and led by model.

The Tyrians quickly devised a strategy to slay the towers. They built a special fire shipthat was loaded down to the aft side to raise the bow. Tyrians struck at the bottom of the mole. Instigating the fire ship the ship jumped up on the mole and set the towers on fire.

Although this was a setback Alexander determined to finish the mole, even though he was more convinced that it would require an impressive navy to take the city. In the end, as luck would have it 120 boats from Cyprus were in the city, as were an additional 80 ships that defected from the Persians. As his naval strength increased, the navy was able to block Tyres two harbours. Fitting numerous ships with catapults and battering rams. He then anchored close to the city. The Tyrian divers jumped out and cut anchor cables. Alexander responded by having the cables to be replaced with chains.

As the mole was nearing Tyre, Alexander ordered catapults to move forward, which started pounding wall cities. In the end, when the wall was breached in the southern portion within the city Alexander was preparing massive attacks. When his navy was advancing through the gap the siege towers were floated against the walls as troops engaged through the breach. Despite the fierce resistance of the Tyrians Alexander's soldiers were able to kill the people, but only those who hid in the city's shrines and temples were protected.

The blood of the besiegers was gushing and, following an extended and bitter battle they did not appear to be lenient. The city was surrounded by six thousand Tyrians were massacred after the city was seized, and another 2,000 were crucified at the shore. An additional 30000 were sold to slavery. He and his household were not spared, as were several Carthaginian pilgrims sought refuge at

Melqart's Temple of Melqart. Macedonian losses were just 400

The siege was finally ended and it took seven months before Alexander could finally offer his final sacrifice to Heracles and held an open torch race, followed by a triumphal parade across the city. Tyre was taken over.

Chapter 7: Alexander In Egypt

After the capture of Tyre, Alexander continued to travel south, receiving surrender of all cities until he was 160 miles to Gaza, a city of wealth that was located near the southern end of the trade route. The city was constructed on a huge mound with walls that were large but they were not able to stand up to the tactics of siege that were developed at Tyre and it was sacked quickly.

from Gaza It was 140 miles from the Sinai desert before reaching Egypt. Alexander maintained a close proximity to the coast and was able to access plenty of fresh water and food provided by the navy that accompanied his expedition throughout the coast. After Alexander was brought to Memphis the city, he was not met with opposition, however the Egyptians have a long history of fighting

Persian rule. Alexander was declared to be the new pharaoh. He also performed offerings to Egyptian gods.

From Memphis He travelled along the Nile towards the coast, which is where he discovered the world-renowned city named after him. Alexandria was to become the biggest city in the ancient world and home to one of the greatest ancient marvels known as The Lighthouse of Pharos and the central point for knowledge and learning, which was the great Alexandria Library. Alexandria. It would be a rich center of commerce and the hub of the development of culture and knowledge.

Then, from Alexandria, Alexander made a long and difficult journey, about 200 miles on the coastline, the 100 miles to the south through the Sahara desert to reach the Oasis of Siwah with a few of his companions. There was the Temple of Ammon was situated there and the high priest would assume the role of Ammon and respond to questions with gestures and nods. Alexander was greeted, by the priest as Son of Ammon was taken inside the temple alone by the priest, and all the other guests leaving outside. After some time,

Alexander was taken out of the temple saying that he was pleased with the answers that were that were given to him, and everyone went home.

It is unclear what information was that were received from Alexander there, however it is reported that he sent an email to Olympias and his mother, stating that he'd only reveal the answers upon his return to Macedonia.

After having left Siwah and later Alexandria, Alexander returned to Tyre in order to finish his goal of defeating Darius and his army, culminating in his victory at Battle at Gaugamela.

Chapter 8: Battle Of Gaugamela. Battle Of Gaugamela

In the 331BCE summer, as it began to approach, Darius had been stationed at Babylon and Alexander was in Tyre. Alexander began to travel East and crossed the Euphrates River, the point Darius was expecting him to follow the river south until Babylon. Instead, Alexander moved across and continued on to the East until he reached the Tigris River, staying to the north of Darius. The reason is because the floodplains were perfect for the cavalry and Darius had a much larger number.

The two King's were a game of cat and mouse neither of them wanting to fight the other, in order to share the territorial advantage. It was Darius who had a much larger army that was costly to feed and even pay for the first time. He moved to the north across the Tigris river, and even discovered an area big enough to permit his cavalry to move freely in a plain near Gaugamela.

Alexander set up camp some miles away from Darius. Even with the reinforcements, Alexander's army had grown to the size of

40,000 infantry and 7,000 cavalry. Darius his 40,000 cavalry and infantry (estimates vary between 100,000 and a million) was a lot larger than the number of troops. This isn't as bad as it appears although the Persian cavalry was a good army, but the infantry was weak and could play an insignificant role in the coming battle.

While on a scouting mission, Alexander came upon an advance party commanded by Darius. While some of the group left, others were detained and were eager to speak of Darius numbers as well as the existence of traps and obstacles in the field.

The night prior to the battle, Alexander was able to convene the generals' council; Parmenio, the commander of Alexander's left flank, suggested that the number of Darius's army demanded that they attack in the night. However, Alexander was not convinced. The historian Arrian has made reference to this event during the book History of Alexander:

It is believed that Parmenio was in his tent and advised him to prepare an assault at night against the Persians and he said that if he did so, they would be not prepared and in disorientation ... However, his reply his friend ... is that this was a way the theft of a win ...

Then, when Alexander addressed his soldiers in the evening, he spoke about the upcoming battle, and reassured that the normally religious Macedonians of the fact that an earlier moon's eclipse was an indication of victory.

The date of the fight 1 October 331 BCE Alexander was believed to have been overslept. Like he did before, he ensured his troops were well-nourished and rested. Darius along with his bodyguards in contrast, spent an unrestful night in anticipation of an attack in the night, but it didn't come.

Alexander configuration was the same as that of Issus, Parmenio was to be the commander of the Thessaly and the allied cavalry on the left predominantly in a defensive capacity while Alexander to the right side of the Phalanx was to command the attack from the Macedonian cavalry.

The battle began and Alexander and his companions immediately began to move to the right of an Oblique Angle. As per Darius's directions Darius's orders, the Persians under the command of Bessus were able to move to their left and fought Alexander trying to defeat the latter. When the Persians advanced further to their left, and then into terrain that hadn't cleared an opening, or opening was made. According to some historians this whole move of Alexander was a ploy. In the midst of the opening Alexander created his troops into a wedge, then swiftly made his way to the left, and into the clearing, and charged the stunned Darius. On the Persian right, the cavalry led by Mazaeus was exerting intense pressure on Parmenio to force him back but the Thessaly cavalry resisted.

As Alexander was fighting the Persians on the left, Darius sent his scythed horses towards the Macedonian center but it did not have the impact Darius was hoping for. The chariots were approaching, and the phalanx simply opened their ranks and allowed the chariots through. The troops immediately swarmed the Persians fighting hand-to-hand quickly followed. Alexander watching Darius was able to seize the opportunity to throw an iron spear at the stunned King (missing Darius by a few inches).

Alexander's march through the gap in the Persian left side caused Darius losing his vigor Darius was unable to fight, and even though the battle was still not lost, Darius took the decision to leave the battlefield. This lowered the morale for that Persian army, despite the fact that the battle was going smoothly, to fall, and they fled with their king and was soon beaten. Alexander had triumphed yet again, and Persia stood in his way. Darius was able to flee Ecbatana in Media had survived , but the king would never be able to lead an army to take on Alexander.

Chapter 9: Pursuit Of Darius

After his decisive victory Alexander was declared to be "King of Asia," thus fulfilling the prophecy contained in the Gordian Knot. Alexander walked towards the south, towards Babylon that was able to open its gates and welcomed the new leader. Alexander restored the main temple of the city and had access to the enormous Persian treasure housed in the treasury. After a rest and relaxation in Babylon Alexander began to conquer the center of Persia. In the month of December 331BC, Alexander was able to reach Susa who surrendered. Alexander received the treasury that contained more than 1,500 tons of silver.

He then moved to the center of the old Persian Empire, Persepolis. Persepolis was adamant and when it was sacked, Alexander allowed his soldiers to pillage Persepolis, without apprehension of palaces. Alexander took over the Treasury that contained more than 1,500 tons gold and silver. He stayed within Persepolis's Royal palaces for four months, to consolidate his financial gains, consolidate his finances , and to determine his next steps. Before departing Perspolis

Alexander destroyed the palaces as a retribution for the destruction that the Persians had caused Athens 150 years earlier.

At the time, Darius was living in The city of Ecbatana (modern Hamadan) and had built up an army of a few hundred in anticipation of troops from the East. Alexander was sent to take Darius in the hope of capturing Darius and convince him to recognize Darius as the legitimate leader of Asia. After hearing that Alexander was advancing against him, Darius fled from Ecbatana towards the northeast. After arriving in Ecbatana Alexander established Parmenio to be the official military commander of the city, which was strategically important. To take Darius Alexander pressed his troops to cover 200 miles in just 11 days, to attempt to fend get him out before he made it over the Caspian gates. After reaching them, Alexander learned that Darius was already through the pass , so Alexander was forced to wait 5 days to rest his soldiers and horses.

After crossing the pass Darius travelled 60 miles in just two days, traversing the edge of the Dasht-e Kavir desert. The next day , as he was scouting in search of food, he learned that his generals had detained Darius. Then, he set off on a final chase, he traveled through two nights through the desert until they arrived at the camp where remnants of Darius's forces had camped out the night prior to. The locals informed them that there was a faster route, via a dry part of the desert , to capture these Persians, Alexander setoff with 500 of his best men. They rode across the night. In the early morning, they covered 45 miles. when he was able to spot the Persians. With only sixty soldiers who were keeping up with him, they fought straight away. When they saw Alexander the Persians attacked and stabbed Darius before running away. At the time Alexander was in Darius the carriage, he was passed away.

He had ordered his soldiers to travel over 250 miles in under one week, which in the past times was unprecedented. half of the horses been killed and the rest were exhausted, but all unsuccessful since they failed to take Darius alive, but Alexander granted him a regal funeral in Persepolis in which he was buried alongside his predecessors. It was July 330BC , and the time was now Alexander became the unbelievably the ruler of Asia with just 26 years old.

Chapter 10: To All The End Of The Earth

After the demise of Darius, Bessus who had been the commander of his Persian army at Gaugamela claimed the title King of Kings and renamed his own name Artaxerxes IV. In Bactria the today Afghanistan the mountain war resulted in no major battle could be fought, so Alexander needed to carry out several smaller campaigns that took three years to conquer the region. Utilizing the discipline and speed that he had developed through the years of battles, Alexander split his army and under the direction of his successful generals, he gradually conquered the region. After several sieges Bessus was snubbed by Alexander who, upon putting him in the road, in chains, naked and with an iron collar, forced him to be mutilated and killed. Additionally, during the battle Alexander was married to Barsine the Bactrian princess who was believed to be among the gorgeous female in Asia.

During the Bactrian campaigns, there was a plot against Alexander's life that was referred to as The Philotas conspiracy. A Macedonian nobleman, Dimnus had a plan to murder Alexander and revealed the plot to his love interest Nicomachus who informed his brother Cebalinus discovered the plot and decided be able to alert Alexander. He encountered Philotas his son from Parmenio and told himabout the incident. Philotas but ignored the warning, believing that this was not a serious matter. Cebalinus continued to work to make his message known to Alexander and, when he succeeded, the two Dimnus as well as Philotas got detained.

Dimnus was able to kill himself before the trial began, however Philotas was a childhood acquaintance of Alexander however, whom was not well-liked by other older Macedonians was discovered guilty and executed. Alexander knew that this would upset Parmenio who was the commander of an army as well as reserves of funds in Ecbatana. The messenger was sent out quickly to the city of Ecbatana. Parmenio had to be executed.

In 326BC, Alexander was at the beginning of his reign and 326BC, Bactria finally secured Alexander the right to carry in his quest all the way to the end of the earth, down to the Indus River and beyond to the modern India. This was more than the Persians had ever been. Alexander traversed through the Indus River in May and entered Taxiles' kingdom. Taxiles who renounced Alexander. They carried to the point of encountering an Indian King, Porus who, instead of accepting the Macedonians made a draw on the eastern banks of the Hydaspes River with a troop comprising 30,000 infantry as well as 4,000 cavalry as well as 200 elephants of war.

Conscient that Alexander was on the way, Porus determined to stop Alexander and the Macedonians in crossing over the river. The Monsoon rains resulted in the river rising and making a direct attack difficult, particularly for horses, who were terrified by the elephants. Alexander removed the majority of his army under Craterus just to the west of Porus and set up three battalions of phalanx further upstream.

Alexander took numerous trips upstream, always surrounded by Indians on the other bank. Alexander discovered an island that was located in the river's bend around 17 miles downstream, which allowed him to cross the river. In the midst of a storm and heavy rains Alexander made the crossing, and then drive away the shadowing forces, which then was able to retreat to Porus who changed sides to confront Alexander who was moving to the to the north, allowing Craterus to move across the river and join Alexander. The battalions that were stationed upstream crossed the river and were able to join Alexander at the time that the battle began.

Alexander created his troops in a standard manner, with the Phalanx being guarded to his right side by Alexander and his companions , with the cavalry of a small number under Coenus which was hidden to the left. Porus put his cavalry to his left side to counter Alexander and placed his main weapons, 200 war elephants, at 15m intervals, in front of his infantry.

The Macedonian Phalanx advanced with discipline, and the Mahout's (elephant drivers) were snatched away and the elephants began to panic and do more harm to the Indians than the Macedonians. In the meantime, Alexander was moving forward with his comrades to try to take out his Indian cavalry. The attempt was not immediate success however Coenus arrived at the Indian army from the left and assaulted the cavalry from behind. The Indians were defeated in a flurry and two-thirds of their troops were killed. Porus was wounded however, when Alexander asked him how he would like to be treated, Porus stated "Like an emperor" and Alexander granted the kingdom to govern for Alexander's benefit.

Alexander moved south to and his trusty horse Bucephalas was stricken with old age. Alexander created Bucephala as a city. Bucephala to honor his memory. Alexander had hoped to conquer the remainder of India and was thought to be a relatively small nation. It became clear that this was not the case , and when the Macedonians arrived at to the Hyphasis River, with the seemingly never-ending country stretching out before them, the soldiers rebelled and refused to go further and giving Alexander his final defeat. Alexander was confined to his camp for three days offering sacrifices to the gods , and declaring that the omens were not favorable, and gave the order that he return to Persia.

Chapter 11: A Return To Persia

In September 326BCE, the forces returned to Bucephala located in the Hydaspees river, and began to move downstream. In his absence , a massive fleet had been constructed with nearly 2,000 vessels comprised of warships, troop ships and supply ships and horse transports. They moved downstream, crossing ever-growing tributaries of Indus river. They fought several people, but in the process of capturing an entire city of Mallians, Alexander, who was the first to cross the walls, was initially assisted by 3 bodyguards. When he did manage to kill a few of his defenders, they were shot by an archer. A bodyguard employing the sacred shield of Athena that was taken out of Troy at the beginning of the battle, was able to shield him from the attack while the remainder of the army could not climb the walls, and believing Alexander as dead, killed everyone.

It was believed in the camp's main headquarters that Alexander had passed away and there was suspicion the generals had been hiding the truth, leading to nearly a riot of soldiers. Even when a letter was retrieved from Alexander to prove that he was alive , it didn't end the rage. It was not until Alexander's body was placed on a river barge , for the army to see , and then his raising of his hands that brought the troubles over to a halt.

It took them until October 325BCE in order to arrive at the mouth of the Indus river, which flows out to the Arabian sea. The army set off to Persia. The army was divided in two, with Nearchus commanding the navy along the coast previously unchartered, Craterus leading a large section of the troops through an easier route to the inland, and Alexander attracted fate by traversing his way through Gedrosia desert. By staying close to coast, and in close contact with Nearchus in order to provide the Navy Alexander traveled through a difficult, dry desert. With temperatures as high as 120°C and lengthy periods with no water, the conditions were extremely harsh. The marching was only night-time for 60 days, and with supplies running low, soldiers were forced hunt for food any animals they could find in their baggage, provided they were not already dead from the heat and had reached Persia in only a shadow of what were prior to.

Chapter 12: Susa Marriages

As the war was winding down Alexander attempted to bring the Macedonian and Persian culture together. This was a practice that had been ongoing from the Battle of Gaugamela but the most awe-inspiring aspect of all this event was Susa Weddings.

Susa Weddings Susa Weddings was a mass wedding that was arranged through Alexander from Macedonia during 324 B.C. within the Persian city of Susa. The goal was to unify his Persian and Macedonian culture by acquiring the bride of a Persian wife and holding the wedding in a large scale with a Persian ceremony, along with his officers to who he planned weddings with the most prestigious Persian wives. The union was not just symbolic, since the new descendants were expected to be the fathers from both cultures.

Alexander was married already to Roxana who was the daughter of an Bactrian chief, however Macedonian as well as Persian customs allowed multiple wives. Alexander himself was married to Stateira who was the eldest daughter of Darius and according to

Aristobulus his other spouse was Parysatis his youngest child. Artaxerxes III.

To Hephaestion the king gave Drypetis the name of Drypetis. She is the daughter of Darius who was his wife's sister. He desired Hephaestions' kids to become his nieces and nephews. To Selecus He offered Apama his daughter Spitamenes the Bactrian as well as to the Companions, those daughters from the more famous Medes and Persians Eighty of them in total.

The weddings were formally celebrated in the traditional Persian manner Chairs were set up for the bridegrooms according to order of precedence. After the toasts, the brides came in and sat down , each with her groom who then took them in his hand, and kissed the brides. The King was the first to marry, as every wedding was celebrated in the same way and, in this particular ceremony the king displayed more than his usual courtesy and camaraderie. The bridesmaids then returned to their wives at their homes, and Alexander presented each bride with the priceless dowry. The rest of the Macedonians who had already had gotten married to Persian women were required to register and they were discovered to be over 10,000. For all of them, Alexander offered wedding-day gifts.

By marrying the daughters Darius or Artaxerxes, Alexander was both being a part of the Persians as well as making his position more secured. He was now able to claim as the rightful heir and son of both former Persian monarchs. Also, he wanted to honour the Hephaestion and make him his brother-inlaw.

What the Macedonians considered of the marriages they had is apparent by the fact that the nobles divorced their wives following the death of Alexander The exceptions were Hephaestion, who died prior to Alexander and Seleucus. Thus, despite Alexander's precedence and precedent, the Macedonians were not more inclined to share the same wealth with the Persians as they were before.

After that, Alexander's faithful companion and second-in-command Hephaestion was killed in Ecbatana from a fever although some sources suggest that Hephaestion may have been poisoned. The accounts of historians about Alexander's reaction generally agree that his sorrow was unaffordable. Plutarch states that Alexander murdered the Cossaeans in nearby towns in order to pay homage to his friend. Arrian mentions that he was the doctor who treated Hephaestion executed because he was unable to heal his. The manes and tails of horses were cut off as to show mourning and Alexander did not want to elevate an additional Hephaestion to the position of chief of cavalry. Alexander ate a diet of no food or drinks and declared a time of mourning across his reign and performed funeral ceremonies typically reserved for kings and laid out plans to construct an enormous pyramid similar to the ones found in Egypt to honor Hephaestion.

Chapter 13: Crossing The Hellespont

B.C. 334

The Expedition into Asia After Alexander's arrival in Macedon the following day, he immediately turned towards the topic of the coming invasion of Asia. He was filled with fervor and enthusiasm to bring this plan to fruition. In light of his youth and the thrilling nature of the undertaking It is a bit odd that he would have exercised the same amount of thought and care in the manner that his actions convey. He was now settling everything in the most meticulous manner in his own sphere of influence as well as among the countries that were within his border, and according to his perception it was the right time for him to begin actively preparing for the massive Asiatic campaign.

Discussions on it discussed the matter with his counselors and ministers. They, generally, agreed with him on his opinion. There werehowever two individuals who were uncertain or, more accurately, who were in actual fact opposed to the idea although they expressed their disagreement through doubts. They comprised Antipater and Parmenio The revered officers previously mentioned as serving Philip with great devotion, as well in the event of the death of their father, their loyalty and loyalty immediately to Philip's son.

The objections of Antipater and Parmenio. Their foresight Antipater and Parmenio advised Alexander that if Alexander were to travel to Asia in the midst of that moment, he would be putting at risk all the concerns of Macedon. Since he was not a member of a relatives, there would be obviously there was no direct heir to the crown. Furthermore in the event of a unfortunate event that caused his life would be destroyed, Macedon would become at the time the victim of rival factions that would soon appear, each offering their own candidates to fill the throne that was vacant. The wisdom and foresight these statemen demonstrated in these ideas were a lot more evident at the final. Alexander died in Asia and his huge empire immediately fell apart and it was devastated with internal conflicts and civil wars over a long time following his death.

Parmenio and Antipater in turn advised the king to delay his journey. They suggested he find an heir from women from Greece and, after that, to return to family life, and oversee the affairs of the kingdom, for short period of time after which, when things was established and stable in Greece and his family had been accepted by his fellow citizens, he could depart from Macedon more securely. Public affairs would proceed more smoothly throughout his lifetime and, in the event that he died the crown would fall without much risk of civil disturbance and his inheritor.

Alexander decides to leave - However, Alexander was completely opposed to any such a policy. He decided to go on the huge expedition as soon as possible. He concluded that he would create Antipater his vice-gerent in Macedon while he was absent, and then to bring Parmenio along with him to Asia. It is worth noting the fact that Antipater was the stateman, and Parmenio the general. That means that Antipater was employed in greater numbers by Philip in civil matters, in addition to Parmenio in military matters however, in the time of Philip every person who was engaged in public life was in some way an army officer.

Preparations Prepared Alexander was able to leave an army comprising about ten or twelve thousand soldiers together with Antipater to protect Macedon. He gathered another army of thirty-five thousand soldiers to accompany his. It was thought to be a little army to be able to handle such a massive project. Two hundred or so years prior to this, Darius, a king of Persia had invaded Greece and a force of 550,000 soldiers, but Darius was defeated and driven back and Alexander was planning to strike back by using a lot less than one tenth of the army.

The description of Thessaly. Vale from Tempe. Olympus. Pelion and Ossa In Alexander's army of thirty-five million the foot soldiers. The remaining five thousand horsemen. Over half of the army came originated from Macedon. The remainder came from south-western states in Greece. The majority of the horse came located in Thessaly that is evident on the map, was a state located south of Macedon. It was actually one large, expanded valley that was surrounded by mountains. The Torrents that ascended these mountains, creating streams that flowed that became deeper but also slow, as they fell into the plains, before merging to form one central river which flowed towards the east and then escaped the mountains' abutments through a well-known dell known as "the Vale of Tempe. In the northern part of the valley is Olympus as well as on the south, there are two Twin Mountains Pelion along with Ossa. There is an old tale of a battle in Thessaly against the giants, who were believed to have been in the early times as well as the gods. The giants heaped Pelion on Ossa in order to ascend to heaven during their battle against their cosmic enemies. The story has led to the creation of a phrase that is used across every language of Europe that explains any extravagant and unusual effort in pursuit of a goal are described as a pile of Pelion on Ossa.

[1]. The chapter begins at the beginning chapter 3.

Thessaly was known for its horses and its horsemen. The mountain slopes offered the most ideal pasturage to rear the animals, while the plains below offered wide and wide fields for training and preparing the cavalry units that were created through the horses. The Thessalian horses were renowned across Greece. Bucephalus was raised in Thessaly.

Alexander's generosity. The love of money Alexander as the the king of Macedon was a wealthy man with a large estate and revenue, which were his personal property, and independent of the revenue that the state. Prior to embarking on his quest the king divided these assets to his top generals and officers as well as those who were to leave and those who would remain. He displayed incredible generosity in this but it was in the end, the drive of ambition, not that of generosity, that drove him to undertake this task. The two main impulses that drove him were the joy of doing good deeds as well as the glory and fame of doing them. Both of these principles are distinct in their character although they are often interspersed. They were the most important and defining factor in Alexander's life and every other human element was subordinate to these two principles. Money was , to him only a tool to help him to attain these goals. The distribution of his estates and earnings as described above was merely a wise use of the funds for promote the major goals he desired to reach and it was an expenditure not a gift. It achieved admirably the purpose that he was aiming for. The people around him all viewed him as incredibly generous and selfless. They inquired about what the he had set aside for himself. "Hope," said Alexander.

Aspects of religious sacrifice and spectacles In the end, everything was prepared to go. Alexander began to honor the sacred sacrifices as well as spectacles and performances that, at the time always preceded big initiatives of this sort. The celebration was grand in honour of Jupiter along with the 9 Muses which had long been observed in Macedon as an annual national celebration. Alexander had now begun to make huge preparations for the festival.

The ancient types of worship. Religious impulses - In the time of the Greeks public worship, as well as entertainment for the public were included in the same sequence of rituals and spectacles. Every worship service was a stage performance, and the majority of shows were worship services. The spiritual instincts of our hearts require the assistance and assistance, whether either real or imagined from the invisible world when undertaking monumental and solemn tasks, and at every crucial moment in the history of. The truth is that the soldiers of Alexander were ready leaving their home and move to a different part of the globe and into the midst of danger and death , from where it was highly unlikely that they were ever to return they had no other kind of celestial security to look to than the spirits of their ancient heroes whom they believed were, in some way or another located their final resting place in heaven on the tops of the mountains. They believed that they ruled, in a way over human affairs. however, this, as small as it may seem to us, meant important to the people. They believed that when they sacrificed to gods of these gods, that they were invoked by their compassion and presence. The gods were engaged in the same activities and filled by the same fears and hopes they hoped that the divine beings they invoked would take an interest in their plights and would be ecstatic about their victory.

The nine Muses The Muses to honor who, along with Jupiter the great Macedonian festival was celebrated, were nine dancers and singers girls, stunning in their countenance as well as form, and captivatingly graceful in all their moves. They came, as the legends of the past from Thrace to the north. They first went to Jupiter on Mount Olympus, who made goddesses of them. Then they moved southward and spread throughout Greece and settled eventually in a palace situated on Mount Parnassus, which will be located on the map to the in the northern part of the Gulf of Corinth and west of Boeotia. They were worshiped across Greece as well as Italy as goddesses of dance and music. In later times, certain arts and sciences are attributed to them like astronomy, history as well as tragedy. There was no distinction in this manner in the beginning.

Celebrations in honor of Jupiter. Shows and spectacles celebrations to honor Jupiter along with the Muses continued for Macedon for nine days, which is the same to the number of dancing goddesses. Alexander prepared magnificently to celebrate the event. He constructed a tent and under it according to legend that a hundred tables could be laid out and he was able to entertain all day long, an enormous group consisting of potentates, princes and generals. The priest offered offerings to these of gods, as believed that it would please the soldiers to believe that they had prayed to. Alongside these feasts and sacrifices there were also military and athletic spectacles and shows, such as wrestling and races. mock conteststhat were fought with blunted spears. These events enthused and increased the passion and enthusiasm of soldiers. It sparked their desire to be distinguished through their accomplishments and led to an increase and heightened need for fame and honor. With a renewed enthusiasm for public praise and relying on the compassion and protection of power that were all they could think to be divine. The troops began to depart from their home country, and bid it a long and, to the majority of them an end of the road.

Alexander's route. Alexander starts his march By following the path of Alexander's expedition on the map in the beginning chapter 3 it is evident that his route was on the northern shores that comprise the AEgean Sea. Alexander was to cross the AEgean Sea across Europe to Asia through the Hellespont between Sestos and Abydos. He dispatched an entire fleet of one 100 and 50 galleys with three banks with oars per crossing into the AEgean Sea, to land at Sestos and then be prepared to carry his troops across the Straits. The army, at the same time, moved on by the land. They had to cross rivers that flow into AEgean Sea on the northern side. However, as the rivers were located in Macedon and there was no resistance was encountered on their banks There was no major problem in crossing the river. Once they had reached Sestos and

Sestos, they discovered the entire fleet awaiting their arrival. waiting to receive their ship.

Romantic adventure - It's quite strikingly reminiscent of the merging of romantic sentiment and excitement with a calm and calculated business efficiencythat was evident frequently throughout Alexander's career as he landed at Sestos and saw it was safe for the vessels to be in place and his army was secured, and that there was no threat to stop his arrival at the Asiatic shore, he went to Parmenio to manage the transport of his troops across the sea and then he took one galley for an excursion of passion and romance. Just to the south of the area that the army was going to cross, was at the Asiatic shore, an expansive plain, and on it were the remains of Troy. Then Troy is the place that was the location of the poems of Homer, which were the source of so much excitement in the minds of Alexander during his early years and he decided to avoid crossing the Hellespont with the bulk that he commanded, to move to the south in a single galleon and then land himself in the Asiatic shore, in exactly the spot that the young romantic imagination was a constant focus and for so long.

The map of the Plain of Troy

The plains of Troy. Tenedos. Mount Ida. Mount Ida. Scamander The Scamander Troy was situated on an open plain. Homer writes about an island in the ocean called Tenedos as well as an adjacent mountain known as Mount Ida. The river was known as the Scamander. The mountain, the island and the river still remain and are still named in their original form until the present however, this river has been referred to as the Mender however, numerous traces of ancient ruins can be found all over the plain and there is no place that is identified as being the location for the town. Certain scholars have suggested that there was never the city of the same name; Homer invented the entire thing as there is nothing concrete in his descriptions other than the river, the mountain as well as the island. However, his story states it was actually a huge and powerful city in the area and a kingdom that was associated with it. The city was surrounded by Greeks for ten years after which period it was taken over and destroyed.

It was the Trojan War. The Dream of Priam's wife. The exposure of Paris The tale of the beginning of the conflict is in large part this. Priam was the king of Troy. His wife, who was a brief time before the day her child was born, sat in a dream that upon his birth, the baby turned into a torch, and ignited the palace. The dream was reported to the soothsayers and inquired about what the meaning was. They suggested that her son was the cause of some horrible disasters and calamities to the family. The mother was scared, and, in order to prevent these disasters, handed the baby to an enslaved person when it was born and instructed him to kill the baby. The slave was enraged by the child's suffering and, not wanting to destroy it using his own hands transported the babe towards Mount Ida, and left it in the woods to be buried.

A she bear, wandering in the forest, stumbled upon the baby, and after having a sense of maternal tenderness towards it, she took charge of it, and raised the child as if it taken her offspring. The child was found eventually, by shepherds who resided on the mountain. They took it for their personal, and robbed the savage mother of her care. The boy was named Paris. He gained beauty and strength, and displayed early and impressive examples of energy and courage that sounded as if he taken in some of the traits of his mother, a fierce and strong woman by the milk she gave him. He was so exceptional for the athletic physique and masculine courage that he not only effortlessly got the love of a nymph from Mount Ida, named OEnone who he later married and also caught the eye of goddesses that resided in the heavens.

Discord's apple These goddesses faced a disagreement that they were able to agree to refer to as. The cause of the conflict was as follows. It was the time of a wedding between them and one unhappy about not having been invited, ordered an apple with a golden color with the words "To be presented to the most gorgeous." The bride threw the apple in the gathering and aimed to cause them to argue over the apple. Actually she was the goddess of discord and, irrespective of the reason for pique in this instance she was a fan of promoting disagreements. This is a reference to this old story that any topic of contention, discussed in a way that is not needed and family members, is still called in the present a fruit of contention.

The apple's dispute. The apple was ruled to favor Venus Three goddesses claimed the apple each of them insisting that she was more beautiful than the other and that was the argument that they had agreed to use to reference Paris. They then displayed themselves in front of his eyes in the mountain, so that could be viewed by him and make a decision. They were not, however, appear to be willing, either or the other to an impartial determination of the issue, however each offered a bribe to the judge to convince him to vote for her. One of them promised the judge a kingdom the other famous name and the other, Venus offered him the most gorgeous woman on earth to be his wife. He opted for Venus and it was not clear if this was because she was qualified to make the choice, or due to her influence due to the promise of bribe the tale doesn't say.

The tale of the bull Through all this time Paris was on the mountain as a simple shepherd and herdsman, never having any idea of his connection to the monarch , who ruled over the city and the kingdom in the plain below.

King Priam however, at this time, in a few games he was hosting in his palace, gave as a prize for the winner, the most prestigious bull that could be found at Mount Ida. After an the examination, Paris was found to possess the best bull, and the King, exercising the power of despotism that the kings of the time had no qualms about showing respect to poor peasants was able to take it away. Paris was extremely furious. The thing was, however, that just a few days later there was another chance to fight with the same bull and Paris disguised himself as the prince of the realm, appeared in the list, defeated each competitor, and then carried away the bull once more to return home in the speed that he could muster.

Paris returned to his parents. In the aftermath of his appearance in court one of the daughters Priam who was named Cassandra became acquainted with the man, and after a thorough inquiry about his story she was able to establish that she was his brother the child who was long lost who was supposed to be executed. King Priam was impressed by the evidence she provided and Paris was brought back to the home of his father. After settling in his new post, Paris recalled the promise made by Venus to have the most gorgeous woman of all time as his wife. He began to find out whether he could locate her.

Paris and Helen

The abduction of Helen In Sparta among the towns in Southern Greece, a certain King Menelaus who was married to one of his brides, a young woman called Helen who was renowned in the far and near by her beauty. Paris arrived at an understanding that Helen was among the most beautiful woman in the world and that he had the right by virtue of the promise of Venus, to claim her, provided he could achieve this by any means. The king accordingly set out to Greece and visited Sparta and formed a friendship with Helen and convinced her to leave her husband and duty to him and marry her to Troy.

Destruction of Troy Menelaus was furious at the outrage. He pleaded with everyone in Greece to join hands to join with him in his efforts to save his wife. They reacted to this request. They first wrote to Priam to ask that he should return Helen with her husband. Priam was unable to grant it and he sided along with his son. The Greeks then gathered an army and a fleet and marched to Troy's plains. Troy and encamped in front of Troy, then continued for ten years fighting it until eventually it was defeated and destroyed.

The writings of Homer - These tales about the beginning of the war amazing and enjoyable they were, weren't the subjects that captivated Alexander's mind. Alexander. The parts of Homer's stories that most captivated his imagination were the ones that dealt with his heroes' characters that fought on one side , and on the other side, in the time of the war, the numerous adventures, as well as the explanations of their motives, principles of conduct, as well as the emotions and thrills they felt in the different conditions that they found themselves. Homer expressed with great beauty and strength the motives behind ambition anger, resentment pride, of rivalry and other motivations that the heart of a human that could stimulate and influence the actions of reckless individuals in the contexts where they were stationed.

Achilles. The Styx. The character of Achilles - All of the heroes whose stories and stories he recounts had a striking and well-marked personality, and was distinct in attitude and actions from the others. Achilles was one of them. He was fiery, impervious and implacable in his character uncompromising and brutal and, despite being unflinching and courageous, he was completely without compassion. It was said to be a river known as the Styx The waters of which were believed to possess the power of making person impervious to danger. Mother of Achilles did a dip in it when he was a baby while securing him with his heel. The heel, having not been submerged it was the sole part that could be injured. Therefore, he was protected during battle and an extremely skilled warrior. However, he argued with his fellow soldiers and retreated from the cause based on a few excuses. He then reconciled , but this time motivated by the same frivolous causes.

Achilles

Agamemnon The Agamemnon Agamemnon was the chief for Agamemnon, the commander-in-chief of Greek army. After a specific victory, in which some prisoners were taken, and later to be split between the winners, Agamemnon was obliged to restore one noble lady who had been relegated to his part, and removed the one who was given to Achilles to take her place. This irritated Achilles and he resigned for a lengthy period from the battle and, as a result of his absence it was the Trojans won numerous and continuous victories over the Greeks. In the long run, there was nothing that could entice Achilles to come back.

Die of Patroclus. Hector killed by Achilles - At last however, even while he was unable to leave on his own, he permitted his closest friend, named Patroclus and who was named Patroclus to wear his armor and join in the battle. Patroclus initially was successful, but he was later defeated by Hector who was the brother of Paris. The incident sparked an anger and a sense of revenge in the minds of Achilles. Achilles renounced his dispute against Agamemnon before returning to battle. He didn't stop his efforts until he had killed Hector Then He cried out in rage and paid his dues by carrying the body of the deceased on the wheels of the chariot along the city's walls. He later sold the body to the father in disbelief in exchange for the ransom.

It was these stories like the ones mentioned in the poetry of Homer with stunning elegance and power, that fascinated the brain of Alexander. The subjects he was interested in were the account of the conflicts of conflicts, the adventures that these soldiers endured, their descriptions of their personalities and the causes of action, and descriptions of the many occasions and events that the wars of the time led and were all designed to draw the attention of a young hero in the martial arts.

Alexander moves to Troy Then he travels to Troy. Alexander determined that his first entry into Asia would be in Troy. The army he led was under the direction of Parmenio and travelled between Sestos to Abydos and then embarked in a single galley travel south. The port was along the Trojan shore , where the Greeks used to embark, and he took a course to get there. There was a bull the inside of his galley, which was to be offered as an offering to Neptune at the halfway point across the shore.

Neptune The god of the sea, Neptune was considered to be the God of Sea. There is a fact that Hellespont isn't the large ocean but is an part of the ocean, and therefore belonged to the thrones that ancient people attributed to the divine power of the oceans. Neptune was thought of in the past as an ancient king living on the seas or on the shores and riding on the waves in a huge shell or, in some cases, in a chariot steered by sea-horses or dolphins. On these trips, Neptune was accompanied by a sea-god gang and nymphs. They were half floating, half swimming, accompanied him through the billows. Instead of a scepter, Neptune carried the trident. A trident is a type of harpoon that had three pronged, as was employed in the past by fishermen in the Mediterranean. It was because of this most likely, that it was selected as the symbol of power for gods of the sea.

The landing of Alexander. Sacrifices for the gods Alexander was the one who took over the helm and then steered the vessel by himself towards the Asiatic shoreline. When he got to the shore the captain took his position on the prow and threw his javelin toward the shore when he was approaching it, as a sign of the spirit of rebellion and hostility that he displayed as he sped towards the northernmost reaches of the world. The first person to arrive at the land. After getting off his boat and offering sacrifices to gods and then went on to go to the sites that were the sites of the events Homer had written about.

Homer wrote five hundred years prior to the time of Alexander There is some debate as to whether the remains and city remains that our hero stumbled upon were the actual scenes from the stories that had intrigued him so much. But he was convinced that they were and was overflowing with pride and enthusiasm while he walked through the ruins. He was particularly interested in the character of Achilles He also admitted that he envied his good fortune in having a person such as Patroclus to aid him in his feats, and having such an author as Homer to commemorate them.

Alexander is on his way to marches - After having completed his journey across the plateau of Troy, Alexander moved toward the northeast, along with the handful of soldiers who had joined him in his galley. Then Parmenio was safely crossing the river along with the bulk of the army that was en route from Sestos towards Abydos. Alexander took them over on their way close to the spot where they landed. To the north of this location, to the left side of the march line that Alexander was marching is the town of Lampsacus.

Alexander saves Lampsacus The present part is left in Asia Minor, although for much of it under the rule of Persia and Persia, was greatly settled by Greeks and, during earlier wars between the two nations, cities were under the control occasionally of one side and occasionally one of both. The city of Lampsacus was the target of the displeasure of Greeks for rebelling according to their words in one instance against them. Alexander decided to do away with the city while he walked by. The people were aware of his plans and sent an embassador to Alexander to plead for mercy. The embassador walked up to him, Alexander, knowing his mission, made a declaration that he was bound in a solemn vow not to honor the request he was planning to make. "I am here," said the embassador, "to implore you to eliminate Lampsacus." Alexander, happy with the zeal of the embassador to give his speech such a rapid change, and possibly impressed by his swearing and vow to keep the city safe, stayed away.

The arrival at Granicus The Granicus was pretty much located in Asia. His Persian forces were preparing to strike him, but it was so sudden and abrupt been his attack that they weren't prepared to confront him upon the moment of his arrival. He moved forward without resistance until when he was on his destination, the bank of the small river Granicus.

Chapter 14: A Campaign Asia Minor

B.C. 334-333

Alexander was held back with Mount Ida and the Granicus - Even though Alexander was safely landed on the Asiatic shore, the route was not quite clear to allow him to travel into the interior of country. He was in a type of plain that was separated from the land beyond through natural boundaries. The south of the plain was a highlands of Mount Ida. From the slopes to the northeast of the mountain, there was the stream that flowed towards the north and into the sea, thus drawing Alexander's army. He was required to climb the mountain or traverse this river prior to he could get deep into the inner.

The Granicus was a thought that it was the easiest way to cross the river. It's extremely difficult to transport a large number of horsemen as well as of heavily-armed soldiers with all their baggage and attendants, over the high elevations of land. This is the reason the army shifted north when they arrived on the Asiatic shoreline. Alexander believed that the Granicus to be less of an obstacle as

Mount Ida. It wasn't a big stream and was easy to ford.

The map of Granicus

Prodromi It was the norm back then, similar to the present time when armies march in a line, to send small teams of soldiers all over the world to investigate the routes, eliminate obstaclesand find potential dangers. They are referred to as in the present Scouts. But in Alexander's time along with in Greek language they were referred to as prodromi which means precursors. It is the responsibility of the pioneers to send messengers regularly to the general section of the army notifying the officers of anything important that falls under their watch.

Alexander was stopped by the Granicus. Council was summoned - In this case, as the army was moving closer to the river the prodromi arrived with news that they had traveled near the river, and they found the entire opposite shore at the point of crossing lined with Persian troopswho had gathered there to fight the passage. The troops continued their progress, and Alexander summoned the top generals around him to think about the best way forward.

Parmenio suggested that they not try to cross the river at once. The Persian army was primarily composed of cavalry. Today, cavalry, while horrible as an opponent on the battlefield during the day, are particularly vulnerable and insecure when encamping at night. They are scattered and eating or lying down. The arms of the soldiers are light and they're not used to fight on foot; and in the event of a sudden entrance by an enemy around midnight in the camp of their troops, both their horse as well as their horsemanship are ineffective and fall into easily to the ferocious invaders. Parmenio considered, therefore that the Persians wouldn't dare be a part-time camper for long periods near Alexander's army should they were patient and the enemy would withdraw and Alexander could traverse the river without exposing himself to the risk of fighting.

Alexander will not give up. His motives - Alexander did not want to follow any kind of policy. He believed that his army was brave and formidable enough move forward, straight through the river, and then ascend the bank on the opposite side, and push to overcome any resistance that Persians could face. He also knew that if he did this, it would cause a huge impression across the entire country, filling everyone with the power and strength of the troops was his to lead and, consequently, would tend to intimidate enemies and ease the way for any future actions. However, this wasn't the only reason he was motivated; he had an even greater motive for wanting to continue his march and across the river and then plow through the massive cavalry bodies along the other side and that was the joy of executing the feat.

The Macedonian phalanx. Its organization was based on this. as the army advanced toward bank, the soldiers moved to organize themselves in the order of battle and then prepared to move forward as if they had no obstacles to their way. The general battle order for the Macedonian army was as follows. There was a specific group of soldiers, fully with arms with a unique fashion, called the Phalanx. The Phalanx was positioned at the center. The men who composed it were extremely well-armed. They carried shields on their left arm and carried spears of 16 feet in length that were pointed using iron that they secured with their hands, with the spears extended far ahead of them. The men were in lines, each one behind one another, and facing the enemy. They had sixteen lines and a thousand men in each line, or according to the military language"a thousand rank" and 16 in line, which meant that the phalanx was comprised of 16000 men.

The phalanx's formidable character. Is incomparable - The spears are so large that, when the soldiers stood in close proximity and the rear ranks were raised close to the ranks ahead, the spears that were spears from 8 or 10 of the ranks were projected to the front and formed a wall of sharp points every one of which was held by the powerful arms of a fit and skilled soldier. The wall was impervious to any force that could be put against it could be able to penetrate. Horses, men, elephants and everything else that attempted to swarm upon it, ran towards their own destruction. Each spear, sensing the force of the strong arms that held it appeared to be alive and was able to dart into its adversaries whenever an adversary was within reach and it could feel for its own fierce hostility that was directed at the spear. If the enemy stood in a safe distance, and then threw darts or javelins at the phalanx in peace, and were stopped by the shields the soldiers carried on their left arm. They were positioned in such a way as to form a set of scales that covered and protected the entire mass and rendered the soldiers almost impervious. The phalanx was, in defense only, and at rest as an army and fortification in one and almost invulnerable. But when it took on an aggressive shape, put it in motion and advanced towards the point of attack, it became incomparably more powerful. It then became a terrifying monster, covered in brass scales, under it, there were 10 000 live, darting points of iron. It moved slowly and carefully however, it did so with an incredible energy and strength. There was nothing human about its appearance. It was a gigantic animalthat was fierce, unstoppable resilient, obstinate, and invulnerable to pain, averse to fears, and striking with a relentless and unstoppable destruction of everything through its path. The phalanx was the central point and the heart the Alexander's armies. It was as powerful and impervious even in the past, it was essentially ineffective on the battlefield of today. Iron balls solid, floating through the air at a the speed of which renders them unnoticeable and swerve through the pikes, the shields, as well as the bodies of the soldiers who carried them, without being able to feel the obstacle.

Divisions within the phalanx. Its location in battle The phalanx was divided into regiments, brigades, and battalions, and was regularly appointed. While the course of marching, it was split into its various parts and, in times of battle, it would be in divisions. It was positioned in the middle of the army in the field. On the sides were cavalry bodies and foot soldiers. They were more light-armed than those of the phalanx. They were able to move with greater rapidity and alertness and perform their duties easily wherever required. The soldiers that were on the sides were known as wings. Alexander himself was used to lead one wing, as well as Parmenio the other and the phalanx slid around in a slow, painfully slow manner between.

The Battle of the Granicus The troops which was organized and organized moved forward towards the river. It was a large and low-lying stream. The Persians were in large numbers along the opposite shore. According to some historians, they had 1100 000 men, other historians say that there were two hundred thousand, and some 6 hundred thousands. But, however but there is no doubt that their numbers were much greater to the army of Alexander and, as reported to be less that forty thousand. There was a small plain to the other bank of the river close to the shoreline and a range of hills that extended beyond. The Persian cavalry was encircling the plain and they were ready to launch a volley of arrows on the Macedonian soldiers at the time they would emerge from the water and try to climb the bank.

The defeat of the Persians The Persian army under the leadership of Alexander of Macedon, entered the streamand proceeded along the river. They were confronted by their foes on the other side. A bloody and long battle ensued, but the coolness, strength and power of Alexander's army won the day. The Persians were defeated by the Greeks. Greeks interfered with their landing, but they reorganized and established on the shore The Persians after discovering that all was lost fled all over the place.

Alexander's prowess. The danger that he was in is his imminent threat. Alexander himself played a noticeable and very active role in the battle. He was easily identifiable in the battlefield due to his attire as well as by a white plume that he wore on his helmet. He was exposed to the most immediate risk. In one instance, you were battling a group of horses that had been chasing him and rushed towards him, a Persian horseman fired a blow at his head using an axe. Alexander was able to shield his head from being struck however, it snatched off his plume as well as a portion of the helmet. Alexander immediately smashed his adversary through his body. Then another horseman, who was on the other side, had his sword drawn, and was likely to be dead Alexander before he been able to defend himself if no one intervened. however, at the same time another combatant who was one of Alexander's close friends who was aware of the danger, swung an extremely devastating blow on the shoulder of the second attacker that it broke him from the body.

The stories are being told. They could have been true and completely accurate or they could have been exaggerations or ad hominem of situations like them that actually happened or been entirely fictitious. Great generals, just like other great men, are usually been the subject of numerous incidents that they do not actually do. It is the particular business of historians and poets to highlight and exaggerate the heroic actions of the great. this art was even in the past as it is in the present.

We should also remember when we read the accounts from these deals, this is only the Greek part of the story we are hearing. The Persian stories haven't come to us. However it was the Persian forces were defeated and, more importantly without the help by the phalanx. The light troops were all on their own. The phalanx couldn't be formednor was it able to operate in this situation. The men, upon surfacing from the water, were required to ascend the banks and sprint towards the assault of an adversary made up of horse teams eager to pounce on them.

The results of the battle. Spoils were sent to Greece the Persian Army was defeated. They were drove out. Alexander was not able to pursue the Greeks. He believed that he had delivered a powerful blow. The news of the victory over the Persians will spread at the speed of winds across Asia Minor, and operate strongly to his advantage. He wrote home in Greece an explanation of his victory, and along with it, was sent to Greece three hundred suit of armor, which were taken from the Persian soldiers who were killed in the field. The armored suits were to be hung in the Parthenon the great temple in Athens which was the most prominent place for them the only place that Europe would be able to pay for.

Memnon was overruled. Memnon was the name given to the Persian general who commanded the battle of Granicus was Memnon. He was against the idea of risking an attack. Alexander was a stranger to Asia without supplies and with no money. He was relying on being capable of sustaining his army through victories. Memnon was, therefore, strongly advised that the Persians would retreat slowly, removing all valuable possessions and destruction of everything which could not be removed, with particular attention to not leave any food items behind. This way, he believed that Alexander's army Alexander was likely to be reduced due to hunger and poverty and ultimately become a victim of easy prey. However, his opinion was to be overruled by the opinions of other commanders and the battle of Granicus was the result.

Alexander attends to the injured Alexander was encamped to replenish his army and assist the wounded. Alexander visited the wounded each one at a time and inquired about the specifics of each one and listened to every one of them who was able to talk. He also gave an account of his experiences during the battle and the way the wound was received. The ability to relate their tale to their superiors and see the general listening with pleasure and interest was a source of excitement and pride. the entire army was filled by the best of excitement, and desire to have another chance to show that they might face danger and even death while serving the leader. In such manners such as these that the beauty of the heart that is Alexander shines. It is important to remember that during all of this time, Alexander was just a little less than twenty-one. He was only a few years old. the age of twenty-one.

Alexander continues his march. The country surrenders to him - from his camp on the Granicus Alexander changed direction towards the south and walked towards the eastern shores AEgean Sea. The nation generally accepted his surrender without resistance. In reality it was not Persian territory in any way. The majority of the inhabitants were of Greek origin and were under Greek but also subordinate to Persian rule. The invasion of the country was merely in the changing of the chief executive officer for every province. Alexander made special efforts to make the people feel they were safe from Alexander. Alexander did not permit soldiers to inflict any harm. He secured every private property. He was the sole owner of the citadels and of the governmental properties was found there and maintained with the same taxes, same laws, and identical tribunals that had been in place before his incursion. The provinces and cities were subsequently surrendered to him as the king walked through the coast, and within a brief period, all of the west of Asia Minor submitted peacefully to his rule.

Incidents. Alexander's generosity. The account of this growth that was outlined by early historians, is complicated by a number of incidents and adventures that add a lot of interest to the narrative and powerfully demonstrate the personality of Alexander and the spirit of the period. In certain places, there could be a battle between the Greek and Persian groups prior to Alexander's arrival. In Ephesus the rivalry was so intense that a kind of civil war broke out. The Greek groups had gained power and were now threatened with a massacre of Persian people. Alexander immediately intervened to safeguard the Greeks, even though they were his adversaries. The wisdom of this act and generosity was widely known throughout the nation, and contributed significantly to the prestige of Alexander's name as well as to the respect of his status.

Omens. The eagle flying over the mast. The meanings of the eagle - It was common at the time for the majority of ordinary soldiers to be affected by what they called the omens, which were symbols and signs they noticed during the flight or movements of birds, as well as others with similar looks. In one instance the fleet that was traveling along the sea to accompany the army's march to land was rounded up in a harbour by the larger Persian fleet that was outside. One of the ships of the Macedonian fleet ran aground. A bald eagle appeared on the mast and remained in the midst of it for quite a while and looked out to sea. Parmenio claimed that as the eagle gazed at the ocean, it was a sign that victory would be found in this area, and he suggested to prepare their ships to go forward to strike the Persians. However, Alexander believed that when the eagle appeared on an agrounding ship which meant they should be looking for their success at the shore. This could always be read in a different way and the savviest generals wanted to find them a way of proving the courage and trust of their soldiers and their strategies they made with the help of other factors altogether. Alexander was well aware that his profession was not that of a mariner and did not wish to engage in battles which, however they may be concluded, he would not be able to claim any glory.

The winter's approach. The newlyweds were allowed to return home. - By the time the winter commenced, Alexander and his army were somewhere between three and four hundred miles away from home And, since Alexander did not plan to travel any further before spring was open when spring was in full swing, he told the army that everyone including soldiers and officers who were married during the previous year could return home, if they wanted to and spent in winter time with the spouses and then return with the troops in spring. It was certainly an excellent decision in terms of strategy because, as the number of people married could not be massive the absence of these people would significantly weaken his army and would naturally populate all Greece with stories of Alexander's courage and energy and the greatness and kindness that he displayed in his life. It was the most effective method of spreading across Europe the most impressive stories of what Alexander did already.

A wedding party detachment - In addition, it could have created an enmity and mutual respect between him and his troops, and significantly enhanced the affection for him , both by the people who left and those who were still. Although Alexander was aware of the advantages of the plan however, no one could have imagined or implemented this plan in the absence of a habitual ability to think about and take into consideration, in dealings with other people as well as the sentiments and feelings of the heart and to have a strong affection for their feelings. The bridegroom's soldiers in a state of joy and delight, set off upon their return to Greece in a group under the supervision of three generals who were themselves bridegrooms as well.

Taurus. Sea passage The sea Alexander However, he had no intention of staying inactive during winter. He moved from province to province as well as from city to city and was rewarded with all kinds of adventure. He started by following the coast of the south, until the end of his journey he arrived at an area in which a mountain chain known as Taurus descends towards the sea, and where it abruptly ends in precipices and cliffs, leaving just a small beach in between and the sea below. The beach was often covered in mud and other times unadorned. There is not much water in the Mediterranean however, the depth of the sea on the shores can be altered substantially by the continuous pressure that is imposed by one way or the other by storms and winds. The water was swollen by the time Alexander arrived at the pass, but however, he was determined to lead his army across it. There was a different route to return back into the mountains, however Alexander appeared to be disposed to indulge the sense of adventure his army had by giving them a thrilling setting of danger. They then scurried along through the cliffs and marched in a manner that was described as at times up to their waists in the water, with the swell crashing into them at all times at the beckoning.

Hardships. The Meander After having achieved a safe passage around this sluggish buttress of mountain range, Alexander turned northward, and pushed on into the middle of Asia Minor. To do this, he had traverse the same range was his first encounter with and since there was yet winter in the area, his troops was, for a period at times, surrounded by snows and storms amid the defiles that were wild and terrifying. They were forced along with the difficulties and dangers that came with the time, to face the ire of their enemies when the tribes that resided in these mountains gathered to debate the passage. Alexander was victorious and was able to cross a valley which flows a river that has given its names to English literature and language. The river that was named known as the Meander. Its stunning stretches of wind through lush as well as fertile valleys was famous that every stream imitating its model is said to meander into today.

Gordium - For all this period, Parmenio was in the western region of Asia Minor with a considerable number of soldiers. When spring was nearing, Alexander sent him orders to travel to Gordium and then, where it was that he was going to, and then meet his companion there. Alexander also instructed that the group that was home upon crossing the Hellespont and returning and proceed eastward towards Gordium in order to make the city the main rendezvous point to begin this campaign.

The tale about Gordian knot Gordian knot - One of the reasons for why Alexander wanted to travel to Gordium was because he wanted to loosen that famous Gordian knot. The history that accompanied the Gordian knot goes like this. Gordius was a mountain farmer. One day , he was plowing when an eagle flew down, landed on his yoke and was there until he completed plowing. It was a sign of good luck however what was the meaning behind this? Gordius didn't know, so he traveled to a nearby town in order to inquire about diviners and prophets. On the way, he came across an old damsel who as Rebecca during the time of Abraham was out to collect water. Gordius began to talk with her and shared with her the event that fascinated him so much. The maiden suggested that he return and make an offering to Jupiter. In the end, she was willing to return with him and assist him. The relationship ended with being married to him and they lived in peace for a long time on their farm.

Midas. Gordius was crowned king. They had a son called Midas. The parents were used to going out at times in their wagon or cart pulled by horses, Midas driving. The other day, they were heading to the town in this manner and at the time it was observed that an assembly that was being held, and was in immense confusion due to the political squabbles and civil disputes that were raging in the countryside. They had been asking an oracle on what to do. The oracle told them the following "a cart would give them a king who would end their endless broils." Then Midas appeared and drove the carriage in the seat where his mother and father were sitting. The assembled thought immediately that this was probably the cart referred to by the oracle and they declared Gordius the king with the acclamation. It was taken the car as well as the yoke as sacred relics and consecrated them to Jupiter and Gordius secured the yoke to the cart's pole using a thong of leather and tied it that was so tight and intricate that it was impossible to untie to tie it back. It was known as"the Gordian knot. The oracle then stated that the person who tie this knot would be the ruler of all of Asia. So far, no one has achieved this feat.

Alexander cut the knot Alexander had a strong desire to look at the knot and see to see what he could do. He took the initiative, and went into the temple , where the sacred cart was placed, and after having a look at the knot and deciding for that the job of dissolving it was insurmountable and futile, he cut it into pieces using his sword. What extent the details of this story are real and what extent they are fictional, is impossible to say; however, the story however, as told, has been passed across generations in every nation of Europe over 2500 years. Moreover, the act of removing oneself from a snag with violence is known as cut the Gordian knot up to today.

It is the Bathing in the River Cyndus

He resumes his march In the end, the entire army was gathered and the king resumed his march. He remained on track for a few weeks and was moving to the southeast and eventually bringing the entire nation under his control, until at last, when he finally reached Tarsus the event that almost ended his life. Certain circumstances made him push ahead with all his strength in the direction of Tarsus and, when the weather was hot and humid, he was overwhelmed by heat and fatigue. In this state, he fell in the River Cydnus to bathe.

Bathing in Alexander's Cydnus The Cydnus is a tiny stream that flows by Tarsus and flows downwards from Mount Taurus at a short distance to the town. These streams are usually very cold. Alexander was immediately struck with an extremely violent chill and was pulled from the water, with a shivering sensation, and finally, he fell asleep. They believed they were dying. They took the man to his tent and when the news of their leader's death was heard throughout the camp, the entire army, soldiers and officers were in the most harrowing and sorrow.

His sickness. Alexander's doctor Philip. There were suspicions of poisoning - A raging and prolonged fever was triggered. in the course this there was an incident that is a striking illustration of the boldness and originality of Alexander's personality. The name of his doctor was Philip. Philip was in the process of creating a certain medicine for him, and it seemed to require several days of preparation. When it was finally presented, Alexander received a letter from Parmenio telling that he had solid reasons to believe that Philip was paid bribes with money by Persians to murder him in the course of his illness and by giving him poison under the guise of medication. It was written by Alexander, stated to be in a position of security against any drug Philip could offer.

Alexander placed the letter on his mattress, and did not reveal its contents to nobody. After a while, when the medication was ready, Philip took it to. Alexander held the cup containing the medicine in one hand while the other handed Philip the letter had been received from Parmenio telling him, "Read that letter." When Philip had completed reading the letter and was now ready to look at it, Alexander drank off the liquid in full, and poured the drink down with the perfect assurance that there was nothing to be concerned about.

There are some who believe that Alexander observed the expression of his doctor while reading the letter, and Alexander was influenced to seek out the remedy due to his belief in his ability to judge the guilt or innocence of the person judged by the appearance of his face. Others believe that the action was a reflection of his faith in the honesty and integrity of his servant and that he intended to use it to be a testimony, delivered in a sharp and decisive manner, and simultaneously, a carefully, that the man was not suspicious of his companions, or easily influenced to doubt their loyalty. Philip was certainly very pleased with the way he had handled things and Alexander was able to recover.

Asia subdued. It was the plains of Issus was subdued. Alexander was now traversing all of Asia Minor, and had conquered the whole country under his rule. He was now moving on to another region, called Syria and Palestine that lies along the eastern shores of the Mediterranean Sea. To get into this new region the explorer had to cross across a narrow plain that was located in between sea and mountains, which was located at the place known as Issus. The place he arrived was populated by the majority from the Persian army and the epic conflict of Issus was to be fought.

Chapter 15: Alexander's Final

B.C. 326-319

Alexander's incursion into India. The army's insubordination - In the aftermath of the events recounted in the final chapter Alexander continued for around two or three years his campaigns and battles in Asia and in the course of these the army encountered a vast assortment of experiences that can't be described in this chapter. Alexander entered India to his feet on the bank of the Indus and, unsatisfied with his progress, was planning to traverse the Indus and then proceed towards the Ganges. However, his soldiers refused to accept this idea. They were astonished by the reports they heard about the Indian armies, including elephants carrying castles on their backs, and soldiers equipped with unusual and unheard of weapons. These rumors, as well as the instinctive desire of soldiers to not leave to a different homeland, led to an outright riot in the army. In the end, Alexander, learning how powerful and how widespread the insubordination spirit was growing, called his men to his tent. Then, after ordering the entire army to gather the camp, he went to meet them.

Alexander's speech to the army delivered a speech to the soldiers where he recalled their previous successes and praised their determination and courage they'd shown so far, and aimed to inspire the soldiers with a desire to continue. They listened to him in silence and nobody tried to respond. This pause of silence was followed by signs of arousal throughout the gathering. The troops were devoted to their commanding officer, regardless of his flaws and shortcomings. They were completely unable to challenge his authority, but they had lost the utmost and unrestrained confidence in his power and virility that enabled them, in the beginning in his professional career to push ahead regardless of any challenges or dangers, wherever he was the leader.

Finally, a member of the troops came to the king's side and addressed the king as follows:

Address given to the man. The army is unable to take it further "We remain unchanged in our love towards you. We continue to retain, and will forever keep the same enthusiasm and the same devotion. We are willing to take you on at the risk of our lives and to go wherever you will take us. However, we would like to beg you, with the utmost respect to think about the conditions that we find ourselves in. We have done everything to help you in a way that could be possible for man to accomplish. We have crossed oceans and land. We've marched through the entire world, and are contemplating the victory over another by heading seeking new Indias that are unknown for the Indians themselves. This is a plan worthy of your strength and determination, however, it's more powerful than us and our power even more. Take a look at these horrifying faces, and see these bodies covered in marks and wounds. Recall how many of us were when we first set out on your journey, and notice how few are left. The few who have managed to escape numerous dangers and struggles are not strong enough or courageous enough to go on with you. They want to go back to their homelands and their countries and enjoy throughout their life the fruit of their labors. Let them forget these desires, that are so normal to us."

Alexander's sadness Alexander's disappointment emotions was a confirmation and strengthened the minds of all soldiers. Alexander was deeply upset and distraught. A small portion of an army could be dealt with by decisive actions, However, when the will to fight is widespread and unstoppable, it's useless no commander no matter how fierce and uncompromising in his temper trying to counter it. Alexander was uncompromising in his refusal to surrender. Alexander stayed two days locked inside his tent, a victim to apathy and disappointment.

Alexander decides to return. He is wounded during an attack. The result was that he resigned his plans for another assault, and retraced his attention to the west. He was a victim of many challenges as he moved on and was exposed to many dangers and dangers, usually in a reckless and reckless manner but with no conclusion. One time in the course of defending the town of a tiny size in the area, he grabbed a climbing ladder and climbed it with his forces. However, while doing so the soldier put himself forward with reckless disregard that his ladder broke and as the others were able to retreat, he was left at the edge of the wall. This is when he walked into the town and was immediately confronted by foes. The other soldiers returned to their ladders and struggled to locate and save the man. A few gathered around him and defended him, whereas others managed to open a tiny gate through which all the soldiers was allowed to enter. Through this, Alexander was saved. However when they brought Alexander from the city, they found an arrow that was three feet long that was not able to be removed from his side through his mail coat.

The surgeons then carefully cut the shaft of wood of the arrow and after enlarging the wound through cuts, they cut out the point of the barbed. The soldiers were outraged they Alexander was able to expose himself in this way in order to put himself in danger and to force them to risk their lives to save Alexander. The wound was nearly fatal. Loss of blood associated by extreme exhaustion. However after just a few weeks, he began to recover.

Alexander's excesses - Alexander's habit of drinking intoxication and violent exuberance of all kinds were in the meantime ever-growing. He did not only indulge in his own excesses but also encouraged others to do the same. He would award awards at the banquets for those who drank the most. One occasion the man who defeated consumed, according to legend around 18 or 20 pints of wine after which he was stricken with despair for three days before dying. over forty other people that were at the same event suffered the consequences of their drinking habits.

He leaves his former friends He leaves his old friends Alexander returned to Babylon. His companion Hephaestion was also with Alexander, and he was with him everything in the sinister indulgences to which Alexander had been attracted. Alexander began to separate himself from his previous Macedonian acquaintances, and bonded himself ever closer with Persian acquaintances. He was married Statira the most senior daughter of Darius and also gave his youngest child to Hephaestion. He favored the same marriages among Macedonian officers as well as Persian maidens as much as possible. In other words the man seemed to be intent on the blending of his characteristics and behavior in the affluence of luxury,

luxury, and vice that was the Eastern world that he had initially was snubbed and disdainful of.

The entrance into Babylon. Amazing spectacle - Alexander's entry into Babylon after returning from Indian campaign was an event of immense splendor and magnificence. Embassadors, princes, and ambassadors had gathered in Babylon from all nations on earth to greet and welcome Alexander, and abundant preparations were made for shows, procession paradesand other spectacles to honour him. The entire country was in a state intense excitement and the most costly arrangements were made to offer an honorable reception to someone who is the conqueror, monarch of the earth, and also the god's son.

Astrologers. Study of the stars When Alexander arrived in the city, it was not a pleasant surprise to be greeted by a group of Chaldean Astrologers. Astrologers were a group of philosophers that claimed at the time to predict human events through the movements that the starry night sky. The movements of stars were observed meticulously in the beginning and in the

Eastern countries, by shepherds who were required to be out outside, throughout the summer months watching their flocks. The shepherds noticed that nearly all stars were fixed to one another, that is, even though they set in succession in the east and, as they passed over them, they set in the west they didn't change with respect to each other. However, there were some stars that wandered between the others in a sporadic and unreliable way. They referred to these stars as wanderers or, according to their culture, they were the planets. they observed their mysterious motions with great fascination and fascination. They were naturally convinced that these movements had a relationship to human affairs and attempted to predict through them the events that would be either positive or negative that were about to strike humanity. When a comet or eclipse occurred, they thought that it was a sign of a terrible catastrophe. It was the study of movements and the appearances of stars, in order to predict the direction of human life is the field of astrology.

Astrologers' warning. Alexander's confusion: The astrologers arrived in a formal and solemn procession to greet Alexander as he marched. They informed Alexander that they had discovered conclusive evidence in the constellations that, if he ventured to Babylon it would be a risk to his life. Therefore, they pleaded with Alexander to stay away from any further, and instead to pick a different city to be his capital. Alexander was astonished by the announcement. The mind of Alexander, affected by dissipation and effeminacy is extremely prone to fears that were superstitious. It wasn't just due to the debilitating effects of violent indulgence on the nervous system that this result was induced. It was also, in part it was the moral impact of guilt that is conscious. Guilt makes men afraid. It does not just increase the probability of actual dangers however, it also opens the mind to all kinds of imagined fears.

Alexander was deeply troubled with this announcement by the Astrologers. He stopped his march and began to contemplate what he should do. After a while, Greek philosophers appeared before him to discuss with him on the subject, convincing him that the study of astrology was not an apprehension worthy of belief. The Greeks did not believe in the astrological system. They predicted future events through the movement of birds or by the appearances made by the dissections of animals as sacrifices!

In the end Alexander's worries were so much quelled that he decided to make his way into the city. He ascended, in accordance, with the entire army and entered with the greatest possible pomp and ceremony. However, as soon when the excitement of those first few days was gone by, his mind began to wander again, and he was stressed, anxious and unhappy.

The death of Hephaestion. Alexander's melancholy Hephaestion was his most beloved personal friend and companion was dead while in the process of marching towards Babylon. He was buried to his death by the illnesses caused by dissipation as well as vice. Alexander was greatly affected by his passing. He was immediately thrown into a state of desperation and despair. It took a while before he was able to over the gloomy reflections and fears that this event brought about. He decided that the moment he arrived in Babylon the city, he would give everything he could to honor the Hephaestion's memory with a grand funeral.

Funeral tributes to Hephaestion So, he sent his instructions to all cities and kingdoms in the area and collected a large amount for this purpose. He had a section from the city's wall taken down in order to create a location for a massive structure. This structure was in a massive dimensions and elaborate design. It was decorated by long rows of prows of vessels, taken by Alexander during his victories, and also by statues, sculptures, columns, and gold-plated ornaments of all kinds. There were sirens atop the entablatures on the roof. They were, through an internal mechanism they were forced to sing acoustic and mournful songs. The cost of this structure as well as the plays, shows and spectacles that were associated to its dedication, are claimed by historians of the time to have been a large sum that, if calculated will be equal to approximately ten million dollars.

An amazing project - However, there were some limitations that Alexander's extravagantness and foolishness. There was one hill located in Greece, Mount Athos, according to a certain projector, it could be cut and formed into the figure of a man, probably with a recumbent stance. A city existed in some of the faults on Mount Athos, as well as a tiny stream, which was a result of underground springs was able to flow down on the opposite side. The person who came up with this magnificent sculpture stated that he wanted to make the sculpture so that the city would be within its own hands and the river be flowing out of the other.

Proposed Improvements to Mount Athos

Alexander was intrigued by this idea. He was intrigued by the name. Mount Athos recalled to his mind the efforts of Xerxes who was a former Persian King who tried to cut a road through the rocks on the northern portion that was Mount Athos, in the attack on Greece. He failed however, he left the incomplete work as a permanent reminder of his attempt as well as the success. Alexander decided that he would not make the same thing. "Mount Athos,"" declared Alexander, "is already the memorial of a king's foolishness and I won't create it as a monument of another."

Alexander's Depression. Brilliant Plans - When the excitement associated with funerals and funeral ceremonies of Hephaestion had ended Alexander's mind was relapsed into a state that was gloomy sadness. The depression, brought on by the stress of previous events due to previous dissipation and vice, appeared to have no solution or relief, but instead led to new ways. However, the traces of his previous enthusiasm remained until he began to formulate incredible plans for the improvement of Babylon. He began the implementation of a few of the plans. The time he spent was in a nutshell, in bizarre shifts: determination and enthusiasm in the creation of huge plans on one hand, and complete abandonment to all insanity of dissipation the following day. It was a painful sight to observe his previous immense soul fighting through, though ever less clearly becoming overcome by the insanity of sin and intoxication. The drama was abruptly ended in this way:

A lengthy carousal. Alexander's excessive behavior - On one occasion, when he'd been up all night drinking and dancing at the bar, guests, as the normal time to break up, suggested thatinstead beginning afresh and begin a new dinner at the conclusion one. Alexander having already been drunk was a warm and enthusiastic participant in the suggestion. The group gathered, as a result, within a short period of duration. There were 20 people present at this feast. Alexander in order to demonstrate how far he had come from exhausting his power of alcohol consumption, began to make a pledge to each member of them each one by one. He then took a drink in one go. There was a large cup, dubbed"the bowl" of Hercules that he demanded, and after filling it up to the top and then drank it down for the good health of one member of the employees present the present, an Macedonian known as Proteas. The feat was received by the business with huge praise, he arranged for the huge cup to be filled with water again and drank it like before.

Alexander's last illness - The work was done. The strength and endurance of his body eventually failed him and he fell to the level of the floor. He was escorted away to his home. The fever was a raging one and the medical professionals tried everything to ease. Once his motivation was restored a little, Alexander aroused himself from his depression, and tried to convince him that he could be able to recover. He began to issue commands regarding the army and his vessels, as if the turning of his attention to thoughts of power and empire could assist in his return from the edge of death towards which he was so clearly taking care of. He was certain to ensure to live.

The last words of his life - He quickly realized that despite his efforts to remain strong and unwavering, his strength was rapidly fading away. Vital powers were wounded and suffered an injury that was fatal, and he soon realized that they were able to sustain themselves but only for a short time. He was able to conclude that he would be dead. He took his signet ring from his finger. It was a sign that he believed that the battle was done. He gave the ring to a friend who sat by his bedside. "When I'm gone," said the man, "take my body to the Temple of Jupiter Ammon, and inter it there."

Alexander's death - The generals who were with him walked to his bedside and after each, they took his hand and kissed him. Their love for him rekindled as they watched him prepare to go home for good. They asked him who the he wanted to give his empire. "To the most prestigious," said he. He was implying, probably, with this denial, his mind was too exhausted and weak to contemplate such a scenario. He was probably aware that it was not a good idea to him to try to control the administration of his empire following his death. He claimed, in reality that he anticipated that the outcome of these questions could lead to some bizarre funeral celebrations after his death. After this, he passed away.

Alexander and Washington the palaces in Babylon were immediately flooded with cries of sorrow at the demise of the prince. This was followed by endless and bitter debates about the succession. It was not the purpose of Alexander's career to establish solid and well-established government in the nations were conquered by him, to foster peace, order and prosperity among people and to bring order and regularity to human affairs, in order leaving the planet in better shape than the one he discovered it in. In this way, his manner of conduct is in stark contrast to the actions of Washington. Washington's intention was to create and improve organizations that could move forward with ease and without his involvement; and he was constantly removing his hands from the sphere of action and control of public affairs, and taking a greater pleasure in the autonomous functioning of the institutions were he had created and protected as opposed to exercising himself, a powerful personal power. Alexander was, on the contrary the other hand, lived his whole life focused on expanding and increasing his own personal power. Alexander was all-encompassing. He wanted to be the same. He did not think about the wellbeing of the nations that he had entrusted to his rule, nor did anything to protect them from the civil wars and anarchy which he knew were likely to break out immediately across all his dominions once his power was at an end.

In the aftermath of Alexander's death . The outcome was exactly as could be predicted. The entire vast area of his victories was, for the long and gruelling years following his death and was the victim of the longest and most intense civil conflicts. Generals and governors each took the power that Alexander's death placed in his grasp, and tried to defend his claim to it against other. This is how the destruction and pain caused by these wars brought to Europe and Asia were resisted for many years during the long and gruelling process of returning to their previous state.

Stormy debates. Aridaeus was appointed king. the midst of a crisis However, following Alexander's demise the generals in his court at that moment of his death gathered immediately and attempted to choose a person to assume the immediate charge. They sat for a week engaged engaging in heated debates about this issue. Alexander had no legitimate heirs and was unable, dying as we've already observed, to name his successor. His wives--if, actually, they can be considered wives, there was one called Roxana who was the mother of one son shortly before his passing. The son was later named his successor. However during the interim there was a relative called Aridaeus was picked by the generals to take over the position. The choice by Aridaeus was a form of compromise. He was not gifted or had any capabilities whatsoever to be chosen by the other candidates for this reason all of them believing that if a man as naive like Aridaeus was the nominal king then he was able to acquire the actual power. Aridaeus took the role however he was not in a position to become king , if not in the title.

The impact of announcement of Alexander's demise - In the meantime when the news of Alexander's demise spread across the entire empire, it brought about different consequences, based on the individual feelings of respect to Alexander and the many individuals and the powers from whom the genius was brought. Many, who had been enthralled by his greatness and the glory of his accomplishments, but not being able to experience the bitter consequences of his actions were grieving and mourning his demise. Others who's fortunes were damaged, and whose friends and family members had been destroyed in the course or as a result to his triumphs were ecstatic in the fact that he, who was such a curse and scourge to many, had drowned, finally before the pious judgement of Heaven.

Sysigambis's death Sysigambis It is believed that Sysigambis her bereaved and divorced mother of Darius is among those who been the most euphoric about the death of Darius's conqueror, but we know that instead she mourned with a long and suffocating sorrow. Alexander was even though the unafraid adversary to her child, a loyal and generous companion to her. He treated her always with the highest respect and care, fulfilled all her desires and contributed throughout, in some way to bring her happiness and joy. The girl had learned to think of him and consider him an unborn son. He was, in actual fact, often called her mom and when she found out that he had passed away, she was devastated as if her final protector on earth was gone. Her life was a constant battle of pain and sadness and the final attack brought her to an final point. She was constantly unhappy and restless. She had no hunger and resisted, just like many who are in great mental pain, to eat the nourishment that her companions and attendants offered , and then pushed on her. At length she died. People said she ate until death, however, it was probably sadness and grief at being left in her last years, in a state of complete isolation and loneliness and without food which killed her.

Celebrations in Athens. Demosthenes In stark contrast to the sad scene of sadness within the luxurious palace of Sysigambis there was an expression of the most raucous and turbulent joy on the streets as well as in all the public areas of relaxation within the capital city of Athens at the time that the news of the demise of the legendary Macedonian King arrived. The Athenian commonwealth as well like all the different states in Southern Greece, had submitted in a very unpopular way to Macedonian supremacy. They were adamant against Philip and refused to submit to Alexander. Their dissent was finally stifled as well as silenced through Alexander's horrendous revenge against Thebes however, the battle was never completely controlled. Demosthenes the orator who exerted such influence on the Macedonian rulers, was banished and all outward protests were repressed. The hostility and discontent remained nevertheless, and was and as fierce as ever, and was prepared to resurface with more violence, at in the moment the awe-inspiring force of Alexander himself was no longer to be feared.

The joy that the Greeks felt. Phocion when, then the rumor spread to Athens--which was at first an unsubstantiated rumor Alexander died in Babylon The entire city was in the most joyful tumult. People gathered in public spaces, and they congratulated and blasted each other with expressions of great excitement. They were in support of declaring the independence of their country and declaring war on Macedon immediately. Some of the elder and more generous advisers, however, were more calm and collected. They advised a few days to check whether the story was accurate. Phocion particularly was one of the most prominent state officials of the city, tried to calm the excitement the crowd. "Do not be too impulsive," said he. "There is plenty of time. If Alexander is dead today then he'll be dead tomorrow, and the next day, there is enough time to allow us to take action with a sense of deliberation and discretion."

Measures of the Athenians True and logical As this view on the matter was there was a lot of humor and criticism to influence the people to whom it was addressed. The people were unified on fighting. They sent commissioners to every state in the Peloponnesus to establish an both defensive and offensive, to fight Macedon. They also rehabilitated Demosthenes from exile and then took all the required military measures to establish and maintaining their independence. The implications of that would have surely been grave in the event that the rumor of Alexander's demise had been proven to be false however, to Demosthenes along with the Athenians the rumor was quickly well-proven.

The triumphant returning of Demosthenes. Great reception for Demosthenes The return of Demosthenes to Athens was like the triumphal entrance of an emperor. When he made his return, he was on the island known as AEgina that is located around forty miles to the southwest of Athens located within one of the Gulfs in the AEgean Sea. They sent a galley for the public to welcome him and then to take him back to the area. It consisted comprised of three oars banks and was adorned in a way to give honour to a person who was a guest in public. Athens is situated a little away from the ocean, and has a tiny port, dubbed the Piraeus near the shore. It's a long straight road that leads towards the town from its port. The galley through which Demosthenes was transported arrived at Piraeus. The entire officials of the religious and civil authorities of the city walked down to the port in a large procession to welcome and greet the exile upon his arrival. A majority of the city's population were on board the train to observe the spectacle and to cheer with their applauses and cheers of happiness.

The funeral was being planned. The final destination of Alexander's body The time had come to make the funeral arrangements were in progress, at a scale of grandeur and beauty. It took two years before they were completed. The body was given first to be preserved, in accordance with the Egyptian as well as Chaldean art of the time, and later was placed in a kind of Sarcophagus in which it was then transported to its home for the rest of its life. Alexander was, as it is noted, had given instructions that the body be transported towards the shrine in the temple of Jupiter Ammon, in the Egyptian oasis and where he was named as the god's son. It seems unbelievable for a brain as his could actually accept this bizarre superstition as the reason for his divine origins and, therefore, we have to think that he issued this directive to ensure that the location of his burial could be a proof of his superhumanity to the majority of the world. In all likelihood, these were his instructions and the authorities that were still in power in Babylon following his death were ready to execute them.

A funeral of an enormous scale was a long and difficult journey. The transport of a body was an ordinary funeral procession created as soon after death as funeral arrangements were made all the way from Babylon towards the western border of Egypt which was 1,000 miles, may have been the most elaborate plan for burial ever devised. It is an analogy in the transport that Napoleon's corpse went of St. Helena to Paris however it was not actually an actual burial, but rather a transfer. Alexander's funeral was a straightforward procession, which took him to the house where the king passed away to the proper burial site--a walk that lasted a mile, it's true, yet it was all within his control. The magnitude of the event resulted in the sheer magnitude of the scale at which everything related to the powerful this event was conducted, since it was just simply a straightforward journey from his residence to the cemetery within his estates, at the end of the day.

The funeral vehicle. Its size and construction is staggering. A huge and intricately designed carriage was designed to carry the body. The stories of the majesty and magnificence of this automobile are almost unbelievable. The staves and spokes on the wheels were covered with gold. The ends of the axles where they were exposed at the center of the wheel, were decorated with enormous gold ornaments. The axles and the wheels were so huge and far apart they were able to support on them a platform or floor for the carriage , twelve feet wide and 18 feet long. On top of this platform was built a grand pavilion, anchored by Ionic columns and lavishly embellished both inside and outside, with purple and gold. The inside was an apartment, which was more or less accessible from the sides, and sparkling inside with precious stones and gems. The 12 feet by 18 inches is an enormous chamber of unimaginable dimensions and thus there was plenty of room for everything that was needed inside. There was a thronethat was moved up a few steps and put back on the platform. It was lavishly embellished and decorated with gold. It was empty, but crowns, representing all the nations under which Alexander was king were placed on the platform. On the other side of the throne was a coffin, which was made according to legend made of gold solid, and also containing, in addition to its body part, huge amount of the most expensive scents and spices that infused all the surrounding air with their scent. The arms Alexander was wearing were set before the throne, and also between the throne and the coffin.

Ornaments as well as basso relievos. Column of mules. On the 4 sides of the car, there were basso relievos which is a term used to describe sculptured figures that were raised from the surface, depicting Alexander himself, as well as numerous military counterparts. They included Macedonian columns, as well as Persian squadrons, as well as elephants from India and soldiers of horses, as well as other symbols of the deceased hero's power and grandeur. In the vicinity of the pavilion there was a net-work or fringe of golden lace, the pendents were attached bellsthat were constantly ringing, creating the sound of a sad sigh, as the carriage travelled. A large column composed of mules sixty-four in total set in sets of four attracted the attention of this massive car. The mules were chosen because of their size and strength, and they were stunningly capacitated. They were outfitted with harnesses and collars decorated with gold, and enhanced by precious stones.

A crowd of spectators - Prior to the procession left Babylon there was an army workers and pioneers were on hand to fix the roads, build stronger bridges and to remove obstructions along the entire line of the road through which the train had to travel. After a while, once everything was done the solemn procession was set to move forward, and then walked out of those gates that led to Babylon. There is no way to describe the massive crowds of spectators who watched its departure. They lined the route as it travelled slowly from city to town on its long and tired journey.

The body was buried at Alexandria - Despite all the show and pomp however, the body didn't make it to the destination it was intended for. Ptolemy was the commander who was the one to whom Egypt was lost during his division in Alexander's Empire, arrived with a magnificent procession of troops to join the funeral procession when it entered Egypt. He decided, for some reason or another to have the body be buried within the town of Alexandria. The body was then buried in the city, and a magnificent monument was built over the site. The monument is believed to be standing for 15 hundred years, however all traces of it have vanished. Alexandria, the city Alexandria is, however, is the true monument of the conqueror that is perhaps the best and most beautiful possibly that any conqueror could ever leave behind. It is a memorial as well, one that cannot be destroyed by time; its character and position are, as Alexander predicted, by giving the city to a continual reconstruction, will ensure its continued existence.

Conclusion

Thank you so much for buying this book!

I hope this book has been useful in helping you discover inspiration from the greatest commander of all time. This book is intended to help you discover the most memorable moments Alexander had during his short life.

Thanks for your kind words and good luck!

www.ingramcontent.com/pod-product-compliance
Lightning Source LLC
Chambersburg PA
CBHW050400120526
44590CB00015B/1761